Y0-AQQ-508

The Nursing
Job Search Handbook

The Nursing Job Search Handbook

Genny Dell Dunne

PENN

UNIVERSITY OF PENNSYLVANIA PRESS

Philadelphia

Copyright © 2002 University of Pennsylvania Press
All rights reserved
Printed in the United States of America on acid-free paper

10 9 8 7 6 5 4 3 2 1

Published by
University of Pennsylvania Press
Philadelphia, Pennsylvania 19104-4011

Library of Congress Cataloging-in-Publication Data
Dunne, Genny Dell.
  The nursing job search handbook / by Genny Dell Dunne.
    p. cm.
  Includes bibliographical references and index.
  ISBN 0-8122-1805-1 (pbk. : alk. paper)
  1. Nursing—Vocational guidance—Handbooks, manuals,
etc.   2. Nurses—Employment—Handbooks, manuals, etc.
3. Job hunting—Handbooks, manuals, etc.   I. Title.
RT86.7 .D86   2002
610.73′06′9023—dc21   2001057398

Contents

Introduction

The Nursing Job Search Handbook is a guide and a practical tool for nursing professionals and those in complementary professions in an active job market. Whether nurses and other health professionals are much sought after, as is expected for the next ten years, or whether nurses are competing for jobs on a tight job market, strategies for an effective job search will be valuable. Whether you are an advisor, aspiring nurse, long-term health professional, or are moving in and out of the health professions, this book provides easily accessible and concrete answers to many of the questions that arise in preparing a career plan or in conducting a job search. My ideas and advice are based on sixteen years of experience in the field of career counseling. I have included specific information that has proven helpful to me and to the University of Pennsylvania School of Nursing faculty, staff, and students as well as health care employers with whom I have worked.

Nursing Labor Market Dynamics

Current market forces affect and shape our health care environment just as they have in the past and as they will continue to do in the future. Nursing professionals have navigated the tides of change and will continue to face change in the twenty-first century. Glancing back at the economic tides that have affected health care, including the nursing profession, may give us a way to understand the inevitable changes of the future.

From the 1950s to the early 1990s, nursing professionals enjoyed a steady demand for their skills, observes Carol S. Brewer in "Through the Looking Glass: The Labor Market for Registered Nurses in the Twenty-First Century," a discussion of the history of nursing labor dynamics published in the September-October 1997 volume of *Nursing and Health Care Perspectives.* Nursing jobs were so plentiful that nurses did not need elaborate job search strategies; employers approached them with job offers. With the introduction of Medicaid and Medicare in 1965, health care promised to become an American right. Health care dollars were plentiful and seemed inexhaustible. Nurses continued to experience a lively market for hiring. In fact, between 1986 and 1992 hospitalized patients with greater needs for acute and technologically enhanced care, coupled with the larger numbers of outpatient and home care clients, led to an increased demand for nursing professionals—and a nursing shortage. There were simply too few registered nurses to meet the demand for care.

Market forces and concerns about the rising costs of health care set change in motion. According to Brewer, by 1984 alterations in health care insurance coverage ended the years of comfortable spending and marked the beginning of the era of controls on health care costs. As changes were implemented, lengths of stay in hospitals decreased, yet the needs of those hospitalized became more acute, requiring new technologies. Patients who in the past would have remained in hospitals were served by transitional, outpatient, and home care services. Even though the number of inpatients decreased, the costs for treating them escalated and the accompanying need for care in outpatient settings rose sharply, increasing demand, and raising overall costs. In 1994, 13.7 percent of the gross domestic product was spent on health care, whereas in 1960, only 5.3 percent was (Bureau of the Census, 1995).

It became clear that relief from escalating health care costs was essential. President Bill Clinton proposed changes to address health care needs in 1992. Since that time, states have implemented changes based on managed care as a means of cost containment. By the mid-1990s, nurses outnumbered professional positions available. This was primarily due to hospital staffing cuts as a consequence of retaining fewer inpatient beds. A combination of cost reduction and a large number of nursing professionals in the educational pipeline, stimulated by earlier shortages, may have added to the imbalance.

Early in the twenty-first century there are urgent needs for nursing professionals. Like tides that ebb and flow, the forces of supply and demand affect the need for nurses.

The Demand for Nursing Professionals

Several factors affect the current increased demand for nursing professionals. The nursing workforce is aging more rapidly than the overall population. In 1996, only 9 percent of the RNs were under thirty years of age. Early in the twenty-first century, over half of the nursing workforce is over forty-five years of age. Experienced nurses will leave the occupation and create openings for younger professionals. At the same time, nursing school enrollments have slowly declined. Some of the decline may be attributed to the misperception that jobs in nursing will continue to be depressed, as well as the fact that some nursing schools have fewer clinical placement opportunities due to less hospital availability.

Dramatically rising numbers of older people, who are far more likely to have medical needs than their younger counterparts, will continue to swell the demand for health care. The U.S. Administration on Aging predicts that the number of people over sixty-five years of age will increase to 53.2 million by 2020 compared to 33.9 million in 1996. These sixty-five-year-olds may be expected to live for an additional 17.7 years. Increased pressure by the health care needs of the elderly population is expected to continue for the next fifty years. Intensive care nursing is likely to increase, requiring more nurses per patient. Patients who leave hospitals earlier than in the past or who undergo complicated procedures in outpatient settings, will have ongoing nursing needs once they leave the hospital. Nurses will also continue to treat many patients with chronic and acute illnesses. Additional sources of jobs in health services for the elderly and the population as a whole will be in the fields of rehabilitation, health and fitness, wellness, imaging technologies, home health care, nutrition, diagnostic services, and prevention.

The American Association of Colleges of Nursing states that most health care services involve some form of care by nurses. In 1992, 66 percent of RNs were employed in hospitals, and by 1996, only 60 percent assumed inpatient care roles. By 1996, nurses pursued work in outpatient settings like health maintenance organizations, public health agencies, primary care clinics, home health care, nursing homes, mental health agencies, hospices, education, research and private practices. The shift continues, and we can expect to see continuous expansion of the role of nurses in primary care, management of chronic conditions and in health promotion and education.

The most recent *Occupational Outlook Handbook*, published by the U.S. Government, names registered nursing as the largest heath care occupation and says that it is one of the five occupations projected to have the largest number of new jobs. Employment is expected to grow faster than average through 2008. The Department of Labor projects that health care careers will be the rising stars of the employment outlook. Jobs in the health care field are expected to increase more than twice as fast as the economy as a whole. Critical shortages in nursing availability are being felt in the marketplace. Economic dynamics and demographics suggest that nursing will be a lively arena in the next ten years.

1
Plan for Success

We all know professionals who seem to have it all. They have reached the pinnacle of career success, are acknowledged by others as experts in their fields, and seem satisfied with their own accomplishments, yet make it all seem effortless. Such people seem unusually lucky; however, most likely the person we admire has created a career plan, worked hard to stay on the path or to get back on, and has organized carefully. Expressions like "you can't reach a goal if you don't have one" or "a formula for success is 1 percent inspiration and 99 percent perspiration" offer helpful hints for development of a career.

If you are a nursing student, a working professional, or a nurse returning to the work force, you are living, and creating, your career path all the time. Design a plan that you mentally refer to each day. Every day offers the opportunity for you to take a step forward.

Develop Your Professional Reputation and Style

For students, every time that you participate in clinical rotations, you have a chance to demonstrate your enthusiasm, competence, willingness to learn, and problem-solving abilities. Go to your clinical experience as well prepared and rested as possible, look professional, welcome challenges, and be flexible. Make it clear that you are excited about your future in nursing, exude enthusiasm, and play an active role as a team member.

Nursing school is more than a time to absorb the basics of the profession. Classmates learn about you, faculty members observe your efforts, and mentors may be developed. New nurses are often hired for their potential, energy, flexibility, and recent training; it is easy to see how active and engaged nursing students demonstrate their leadership potential. Your professional reputation starts here.

For seasoned professionals, each day that you report to your workplace or volunteer roles, you have the opportunity to demonstrate your enthusiasm, competence, and willingness to assume new challenges. Show that you are a lifelong learner. Approach each day with the same excitement and energy as the first day you were on the job. Be visible, demonstrate your abilities and knowledge, and be a positive presence. Your professional reputation is a work in progress.

Garner Experience Along the Way

Nursing degree candidates in all programs are well served by acquiring experience as they work toward program completion. It is a challenge to get your first clinical position with no experience—you must have experience to get experience.

After completing one semester of clinical training or completing two years of a baccalaureate nursing program, undergraduates should consider working in clinical health care settings on a part-time basis. Clinical facilities seek trainees for special programs (sometimes referred to as extern programs, training programs, or associate programs) for part-time staffing or for the summer. Once you have completed a few clinical courses, you are more likely to be hired. Availability of programs is usually determined by need and, on a year-by-year basis, according to the budget. Any clinical or patient-related experience is helpful for your future as a nurse.

Organized for student nurses, extern programs often involve ongoing education and perhaps mentoring; the term extern may be daunting, however, to an employer that cannot afford such an organized program. It is best to inquire about part-time clinical or summer jobs unless you have learned that the facility has offered an extern program in the past.

Check with your hiring organization or the state to see if certification is required for summer jobs that interest you. Most states do not require that current full-time nursing students, who will work a maximum of three months, earn the certification. Some organizations require certification of unlicensed personnel. States vary as to the terminology and certification requirements for summer employees. Inquire about certification with your preferred summer employers, especially in nursing homes that receive Medicare payments. Nursing assistant or nurse aide certification requires completion of a training program and an exam.

As a student employee, accept a position only if there is a clear job description. Be certain that the employer provides training for components of the job that you are not yet comfortable with or for which you are not qualified. If you are asked to do more than you should, or more than your job description includes, discuss it with your supervisor first, as she/he is required to know what is appropriate for unlicensed workers and should adhere to your job description. If your concerns are not addressed at this level, contact the director of your official program or a nursing liaison for further information about appropriate ways to implement safe practices for you and for patients.

In the senior year, some baccalaureate nursing programs offer students the opportunity to elect specialized courses leading to certificates (e.g., IV insertion or EKG interpretation). Take advantage of all the skill-based clinical coursework and experience available to you and let potential employers know about it.

Work experience benefits students in master's or combined bachelor's/master's programs as well. Those who have work experience in their areas of interest find the job search more manageable (see Chapter 7).

Demonstrate Abilities for New Roles

For seasoned professionals, whether it is projects that you complete in advanced classes, jobs you have held, or responsibilities you have assumed at work or with charitable and professional organizations, experience tells a potential employer what you can do for them. If you wish to change roles or careers, it is important to demonstrate that you have skills in the new field. Coursework, special assignments, leadership roles, committee service, and volunteer commitments may offer experience in a field or area of expertise that clarifies your abilities to fulfill a new role.

Assume School or Professional Leadership

Opportunities to contribute and excel exist outside clinical settings and classrooms as well. Leadership opportunity through the Student Nurses Association or university-wide organizations may also set you apart from other nurses and demonstrate your potential, as well as strengthening your list of personal and professional accomplishments.

Opportunity to lead, and be noticed for your accomplishment exists outside the workplace as well. Contributions to professional organizations as office holder, committee person, presenter, or active participant may earn acknowledgment from colleagues and offer the chance for you to assume leadership.

Work as a Volunteer

Extra-professional activities, like community service, demonstrate your energy and leadership. You may be a scout leader or mentor for an inner-city student. Messages about how you spend your extra time may be significant to potential employers and give clues about what kind of person you are. Involvement in the world outside school or work offers insight about what you will contribute in the future.

Clarify Your Credentials with Licenses and Certifications

Your credentials for and expertise in any given field may be judged by licenses and certifications earned. No matter what your area of interest, speak with professionals in your field of interest to determine what credentials may be necessary or advantageous.

Passing the board exams after completing your program of study earns graduates the coveted title of registered nurse. Most nurses happily remember when they added the RN after their name. For information about the National Council License Exam (NCLEX) see (www.ncsbn.org/public/testing/testing_index.htm).

Nurses are licensed in the state in which they took the board exams. Becoming licensed in other states requires a contact with that state's board of nursing to complete the paperwork for licensure. Fees for this processing vary by state (between $60 and $200). The National Council of Boards of Nursing (www.ncsbn.org/contact_us.html) lists state board addresses, fees, and licensure information. States vary in their requirements for nursing licensure, so begin the paperwork early. Your department or school or professional organization will provide you with detailed information about this. Web sites like www.nursingcen ter.com/career/licensure.cfm also facilitate a quick search for state licensure contact information.

For registered nurses and advanced practice nurses, certifications verify your educational preparation and demonstrate your competency in specialized areas of practice. Certification is based on your educational attainment, or current expertise, as defined by certifying organizations like the American Nurses Credentialing Center (ANCC) (www.nursingworld.org/ancc/index.htm#cert). The appendix lists credentialing organizations. Before getting too far into the job search, make certain you know what certifications and licenses are necessary to obtain employment in your field and location of choice.

Organize Your Paperwork

Keep certification information, license numbers, health test results (immunizations, etc.), security clearances, letters of recommendation or list of names of those who will recommend you, transcripts, class descriptions, degrees, awards, thank-you letters, letters of acknowledgment, professional writings, list of presentations, professional evaluations, and other relevant professional documents in one place. Include your resume or curriculum vitae, cover letters, list of networking contacts, dates for follow-up, job application copies, and contracts. You may be asked to provide one of these documents on very short notice, or you may simply be relieved to have them handy for your own reference.

Request Letters of Reference

Potential employers request letters of reference when they are in the process of making hiring decisions and will certainly require recommendations for their files before you are hired. Months before you need then, request letters of reference from those who will write on your behalf. Keep copies of general references so that you can simply and quickly send them to potential employers. If you have just completed a course of study, ask faculty members and several clinical instructors for general letters of recommendation about your clinical abilities. It is most efficient to request general letters about your competencies so that the letters may be used for multiple potential employers. Nursing schools often store letters of reference for their students and alumni and send letters to potential employers at the student's request. When possible, keep copies of your letters of recommendation.

If you are currently working and do not yet wish for your employer to know that you are seeking a new job, you can use letters of reference from previous positions or give permission for previous employers to be contacted. You may also offer permission for your current supervisor to be contacted once you have shared your job search information with current colleagues.

Discuss, in advance, your interest in calling on professional colleagues as references. Whether you solicit actual letters of reference, list their contact information on applications, or give permission for them to be called or contacted in any way, it is professionally courteous to request permission in advance.

If in doubt about the quality of a reference, retain your right to read the letter of recommendation or choose another writer. In addition, you may wish to ask the potential referee, in advance, if he or she feels comfortable giving you a positive recommendation.

Package Your Credentials

Bring your background of successful work experience, academic credentials, list of references, certifications, and contributions outside work together in a usable package. Prepare an up-to-date resume and have it on hand; keep the basic supporting documents with it. This grouping of facts and record of experiences is a positive package and may boost your confidence as you move forward in a job search or career change. Base written materials and interview preparation on the facts in hand and create a powerful professional presentation. This preparation will also help you to recognize your many gifts, related experiences, skills, and accomplishments and help you establish language to describe them. Even if you are satisfied in your workplace, or have a job offer, you may be asked from inside or outside your own organization, on short notice, for a resume and letters of reference. Keep them up-to-date and know where to find them.

Understand the Hiring Process

Students completing nursing programs will not be officially or permanently hired as RNs until you have passed the board exam. Prepare for the NCLEX (www.ncsbn.org/public/testing/testing_index.htm), let the employer know your test date, and apply for positions before you take the exam. When nurses are in demand, you may get a job before passing the exam. Some organizations will hire a recent graduate of a nursing program as a Graduate Nurse (GN). In some states, you may apply for a temporary practice permit from the state board to work on a contingency basis. Once you pass (become licensed), you can be officially hired as an RN.

Be aware that large health organizations may offer system or specialty orientations only on a monthly, biweekly, or weekly basis. You begin the system orientation, which is necessary to start work, when you pass the board exam. Unit orientations and preceptorships may be six to eight weeks in length once you are assigned to a specific work area.

Health facilities hire nurses as needs arise in particular units and as budgets allow. Nurse recruiters presently report steady needs for nurses in medical surgical units and in intensive care units. Agency budget cycles affect their hiring ability, as well.

During periods when the demand for nursing professionals is great, hiring may take place very quickly. Employers may woo nurses in various ways. Under these circumstances, be certain that you take plenty of time to consider all aspects of a job offer. Make a choice that will allow you to grow and flourish as a professional.

Under usual circumstances a job search may take several months from start to finish. Even after a potential employer has acknowledged receiving your application or resume and has expressed interest in your candidacy, time may elapse before a meeting is planned. Also allow time for a hiring process that includes several levels of meetings. In large organizations, human resources departments receive applications for all jobs and may pass a nursing candidate's paperwork along to a nurse-recruiting specialist. Others encourage nursing candidates to contact the nurse recruiter directly. A nurse recruiter will meet you for a screening interview to determine if you are a good candidate for positions in their organization. If an appropriate position is available, you may be referred to a clinical nurse manager, or the equivalent, who is the first of those you have met with hiring authority.

Once you have met a nurse manager, you will probably be required to meet others in the unit or practice group. Once a hiring decision is made and an offer tendered, it may take time for you to make a decision once the facts are in your hands. Additional steps before hiring may include a physical or even a security clearance in addition to the completion of standard paperwork.

Several levels of meetings are usually required before hiring takes place in medical practices outside large medical systems as well. Once you have made an approach and have been invited to come for an interview, the business manager may be the first decision-maker you encounter and meetings with other team members will follow. As other candidates may also be under consideration, you may not hear back from the prospective employer for some time. And even once a job offer is made, paperwork (including licensure if you are moving to another state) and negotiations about salary and benefits may precede hiring.

For high-level positions requiring a master's degree, count on a more extended job search. As you reach more specialized areas of practice, jobs are fewer, and competition may be greater. Keep in mind that the job search process is sometimes protracted and takes many steps. Prepare in advance for a greater commitment of time in a search for advanced practice, administrative, or other specialized positions. You may have little control over the process and its timing (see Chapter 2 on "Job Search Strategies" to learn how to shorten the process).

Even if it is several months before you wish to change jobs, complete your program, or take your board exam, you should prepare for your job search by clarifying your own preferences and researching some basic questions. It is never too early to determine what region, under what circumstances, and with what sort of employer you wish to practice. Your early research will facilitate the actual job search and transition to a new position. Job changers should also allow ample time for networking and preparation. Patiently lay the groundwork, work toward your goal every day in a systematic way, engage others, and prepare to count yourself among the lucky.

2
Job Search Strategies

Whether you are looking for a full-time, part-time, or summer position, a job as a staff nurse, advanced practice nurse, or administrator or a related health care position, the following strategies will apply. There are many ways to conduct a job search, with some combination being the most effective. In planning your strategies you should identify several methods that you can implement simultaneously. Your primary goal is to tell as many people as possible that you are looking for a job. Concentrate on disseminating this information in a professional and appropriate manner.

Network: Tap the Hidden Job Market

Alumni report that they found their jobs through some type of networking. What exactly does networking mean? Basically tell *everyone* (and that means everyone—parents' friends, religious advisors, your dentist, neighbors, etc.) you know that you are looking for employment. Explain your preferences; seek their advice. Find out if they know of anyone else you should speak to. Inform your colleagues at work, faculty members, supervisors, other mentors, and professional acquaintances of your interests and hopes for the future. Ask their advice and counsel. If an employer with a vacancy hears of a qualified candidate from someone they know and respect, they will most often want to interview and consider the individual even before advertising the position. This is the "hidden job market."

Develop a Self-Talk

Develop a short self-talk so that when you meet someone for the first time, you can tell them enough about yourself and your interests to join in your efforts. At a professional conference, on the job with patients or other professionals, in a social situation, or on a train ride, you may have a one-minute opportunity to share information about yourself and your goals. Instead of responding to "where are you from?" with "the University of Washington," try giving a more expansive answer: "I'm about to complete the Family Nurse Practitioner Program at the University of Washington, and I'm on my way to meet with a representative of the National Public Health Service about a position with them. I'd like very much to serve women and children in rural areas. I'm getting off in Pittsburgh, and I'll travel from there to a site in West Virginia." The listener has learned some important facts about you and about your goals. When you try the sixty-second self-talk, you will be surprised at how many people have something to add, offer to help you, provide advice, or know someone who can help you.

Locate Contact Information

To facilitate your networking efforts, many schools of nursing maintain a list of alumni who may volunteer to be informational sources to other alumni and current students. These alumni can be invaluable in discussing potential employers and organizations or in providing leads and tips. When you contact one of these alumni, or anyone else for that matter, ask to arrange a time for an informational interview.

There are other ways to locate potential contacts. Professional associations often maintain lists of members or offer directories with member contact information and may also have online contact information for members. Some nursing school libraries, public libraries, or university career libraries have books that list groups of specialty practices or organizations. Directories, such as the *Directory of Nurse-Midwifery Practices* (Washington, D.C.: American College of Nurse-Midwives, 1999), *Guide to the Nation's Hospices* (S. Deerfield, Mass.: National Hospice Organization, 1999), *Directory of Management Consultants* (Fitzwilliam, N.H.: Kennedy Publications, 1998), and *Hoover's Directory of Human Resources Executives* (Austin, Tex.: Hoover's, 1996), and *Plunkett's Health Care Industry Almanac* (Galveston, Tex.: Plunkett Research, 1997) offer individual names or organizational names and contact information.

Online resources offer great opportunity for contact information. Web links offer individual and organizational information like White Pages at www.theultimates.com and Yellow Pages at www.switchboard.com. Find email addresses at www.whowhere.lycos.com, email listservs at www.liszt.com, and news groups at www.deja.com. Medical World Search (www.mwsearch.com) may also be helpful, as it is a search engine specifically designed for the medical field. Utilize a variety of resources to identify contacts in your field.

Interview for Information

It is a good idea to conduct informational interviews with people employed in positions, practices, facilities, or agencies that are of interest to you. The purpose of the meeting is to learn more about a career field, job title, or organization, as well as to connect with another person who may offer advice. This is often difficult for job seekers to do. It is worthwhile to keep in mind, however, that many people enjoy helping others, sharing information, and being in a position to give advice. Professionals who have recently accepted their positions are often most inclined to offer assistance to others since they have recently been through the job search process themselves.

Networking requires initiative and forethought. If you are planning to enter a field in which you have had little prior experience, your first step should be to learn more about the field. Refer to resources like home pages and printed literature to get the feel for a field or organization before approaching an individual for information. Call or email people who hold positions or work in organizations that seem interesting to you to seek a time to talk with someone about the organization or practice. If you write, state clearly why you would like to talk with them, express your interest in their field, job title, or organization, and enclose a resume so the recipient understands a little bit about your background. Request a fifteen-minute appointment, or a telephone interview if it is not possible to meet, to discuss the organization and an employee's career path. Keep to the agreement of fifteen minutes since this busy person is doing you a favor. Prepare some well thought-out questions to keep the conversation going and to gain the information that you are seeking (see sample questions for networking).

Dress in professional attire. Remember, you want to impress a potential employer with your professionalism and degree of initiative and preparedness. At the end of an informational interview you should always ask for names of other people you can speak with to gain more information about the field. This is networking. Promptly send a thank-you note to the person who shared this time with you. If you were impressed by the organization, you can mention that fact in the letter and state that you are enclosing a resume should a position become available.

Sample Networking Questions

? Tell me about your background, career progression, etc.

? You are called a quality assurance specialist (staff writer, nurse manager, pharmaceutical rep, trainer, education specialist). How would you describe your responsibilities day-to-day?

? What would a typical day be like for you?

? What skills do you feel you use most often? How has your nursing background benefited you?

? How did you make the transition from clinical work to administration?

? How did you approach your search when you changed from hospital management to health care consulting?

? In this field/position what are your most prominent rewards and biggest frustrations?

? When you hire new people, what criteria do you use?

? When you have a vacancy, how and where is it advertised?

? Are there professional associations or publications you would recommend that would expand my knowledge of this field?

? What other career areas are related to your work?

? How would you advise me to prepare myself for entry into this field/ organization?

? If I look for work in this field, where would you suggest that I look first?

? Is there anyone else who you recommend that I talk with?

Respond to Advertised Positions

Newspaper Classified Ads

Did you know that only about 10–15 percent of all jobs are advertised in newspapers? This means that people miss most opportunities when they use only this means of job searching. This doesn't mean that you should stop buying the paper; it just means that you shouldn't limit yourself to this method and expect to be employed quickly.

When you do apply for a job from the newspaper, make an effort to locate the name of the appropriate person to whom you should direct your cover letter and resume. With the organization, for example, you can locate a web page that may have a staff list to help you identify the department or unit head. Another approach is to make a phone call to ask who manages a practice or who chairs the hiring committee. This will take work but will give you an edge over your competitors. If the person designated to receive the resumes is someone in personnel, try to determine to whom you would report if hired. Send an additional copy of your resume and a cover letter to this individual to enhance your exposure.

Look Beyond the Want Ads

Read articles to gather information about the job market, openings of new facilities, or new high-level administrators. You may extrapolate from your readings that new employees will be needed in the near future, creating an opportunity to be in the right place at the right time and of being well informed. To locate articles that pertain to your specific areas of interest, refer to resources like Excite's NewsTracker (www.excite.com) to select daily news from more than three hundred online newspapers and magazines.

Professional Journals

Many interesting jobs nationwide are advertised in professional journals. Many professional journals have online versions. In addition to responding to publicized ads in journals, read between the lines of articles in order to get a feel for the current news in many different aspects of your field. If you see that an organization is about to expand, it is likely that they will need to hire new staff. If you see that a certain individual has written about and is involved in an area of interest to you, you may want to try to obtain an informational interview with that person. Design your cover letter to express your anticipation of their staffing needs and provide them with information about you and your abilities before they even start advertising.

Find Listings of Jobs Through as Many Sources as Possible

Many university career offices serve students and alumni by providing job listings. Similarly, many university academic departments post their own listings. Professional organizations such as the American Nurses Association, may have job registries for members and generate regular listings. Federal, state and city governments may also have regular listings to which you may subscribe. Nursing periodicals, such as *The Nursing Spectrum* (King of Prussia, PA), advertise vacancies, as do discipline-specific periodicals like *Quickening*, the bimonthly publication of the American College of Nurse-Midwives. To learn more about online job listings see "Use Electronic Resources" below.

Research and Contact Employers

Send cover letters and resumes to employers that are of specific interest to you because of the services that they offer or their reputation in the field. Call or check the web pages of organizations to get the name and title of the appropriate person to whom to send the information. For names of organizations, university libraries, career service libraries, and public libraries have various directories listing professional employers and organizations nationally and worldwide. The Internet offers easy access to this information as well. Refer to the sections below on long-distance job searches and using the Internet.

It may be most effective to call a hospital or peruse information from the web to learn about the application process, open house dates, or deadlines. For staff nurse positions, applications are almost always required. Avoid getting caught in the "paper chase" and consider submitting an online application (see "Use Electronic Resources" below).

In hospitals and other medical facilities, it is always a good idea to meet the nurse recruiter; describe your interests and send your resume along with a cover letter referring to the reason you would like to work in this particular organization. You may be identified by a nurse recruiter as a good candidate for a particular job and be referred to a nurse manager. The decision-makers are often the nurse managers of individual floors, units, or departments and the office managers of outpatient practice groups. In order to have your qualifications seen directly by decision-makers, you may wish to learn who manages the unit that interests you and forward a resume and focused cover letter directly to that unit manager. If you know other nurses who work on a floor that interests you, send them a copy of your resume and letter of interest as well.

Make contact with potential employers via email, telephone, or letter. Targeted letters should be specific about your interests and professional goals, as well as your reasons for contacting the organization; they may include your intention to follow up by phone. Gain as much information as possible about the organization beforehand by looking in libraries, talking to faculty/professionals in the field, and requesting literature from the public relations department, identifying people within the organization for informational interviews, or viewing web pages such as Hospital Web: http://neuro-www.mgh.harvard.edu/hospitalweb.shtml.

Undertake a Long-Distance Job Search

For a host of reasons, recent nursing graduates and practicing nursing professionals may choose, or need to seek, positions outside their current regions. There are logistical challenges associated with a job search from a distant location. There are also many practical hints and resources that can assist you in making a smooth transition to work in another city or area.

Research Your Target Area

Make sure that the type of work setting that you want is available and that you will be able to afford housing. Web sites may be helpful. Calculate the differences in the cost of living between cities at www.homefair.com/homefair/cmr/salcalc.html, http://verticals. yahoo.com/cities/ and the Cost of Living Index at Expat Forum (www. expatforum.com/Resources/icol.htm). The web sites allow you to enter a salary offer from one location and calculate an equivalent salary for another. For example, if you are moving from Chicago to Hartford, Connecticut, you can expect that $59,000 in Hartford will be roughly the equivalent of your $100,000 salary in Chicago. In addition to salary comparisons, the sites invite you to search for information about moving costs, communities, cities, schools, and real estate. In its Moving Network section, *Nursing Spectrum* offers complementary information at www.nursingwebsearch.com.

Other sites offer personal assistance to facilitate successful moves. Relocation assistance is offered at www.virtualrelocation.com. This Virtual Relocation site offers side-by-side statistical comparisons of your present and potential hometowns. Find an apartment through Spring Street at www.springstreet.com and RentNet at www.rentnet.com or a house through www.Realtor.com.

Web sites provide information about potential employers nationwide. For links to hospitals, health care systems and health organizations in the United States and abroad check http://neuro-www.mgh. harvard.edu/hospitalweb.shtml. Explore web sites like these to locate possible employers in your new area: Directory of Healthcare Services (www.dorlandhealth.com.directories.htm), Elder Connect (www.elder connect.com/), National Hospice Organization (www.nho.org), and the Continuing Care Accreditation Commission (www.ccaconline. org). Other web sites associated with the U.S. Department of Health and Human Services (www.os.dhhs.gov) offer information to consumers that contain lists of long-term care facilities in different regions. See "Use Electronic Resources" below for broad-based job search web sites as well as those that are specific to health care. With a little research, you can get a feel for the new community. Read local publications from your target area. Try Career Path (www.careerpath.com) for searchable classifieds from most major metropolitan newspapers. For news from your target area, check your library for major newspapers. Many newspapers have online editions.

Check with your alumni office or professional association to see if there is an alumni club or professional group meeting regularly in the new area. Attending a club or professional meeting is a good way to meet many people, who, in turn, can introduce you to others.

Use a local telephone directory or other written materials. A nationwide microfiche collection of phone books is available at many large libraries. You can purchase your own phone directory from the phone company. You can also find numbers online. Good sources are www.switchboard.com and www.teldir.com/eng. For an excellent compilation of online and published information and resources, take a look at *Health Care Jobs Explosion!* by Dennis V. Damp (Amherst, N.Y.: Advanced Educational Products, 1998). Other written materials that may be helpful are *Best Hospitals in America* by John Wright (Chicago: Gale Group, 1995), *Washington DC Health Groups Directory* (Washington, D.C.: National Health Council, 1999), *New York City (Greater) Cares Directory: Guide to Social and Health Services* by United Way of New York City (Dorland's Directories, 1999), and the *Human Care Services Directory of Metropolitan Chicago* (Huntingdon Valley, Pa.: Morgan Rand, 1999). Another good series is the *Book of Lists*; many major cities produce an annual *Book of Lists* that includes their largest industries. For example, the *Philadelphia Business Journal* publishes a *Book of Lists* that names and offers contact information for its pharmaceutical companies. The *Books of Lists* are often in libraries.

Learn more about the city through local organizations. Many cities sponsor job fairs. Contact the local Chamber of Commerce to find out whether a job fair is offered in the area of interest to you. The Chamber of Commerce may also publish directories or enable you to reach local chapters of professional associations. The United Way often has good information on local not-for-profit organizations.

Demonstrate Your Commitment to Relocating

If you have connections to the part of the country that interests you, stress them on your resume or mention them in your cover letter. If not, you may need to overcome employers' doubts that you will make the move if offered the job. Many employers are favorably impressed with a student who grew up in an area, has gone away to school or has worked in other areas, and wants to return home. If you want to relocate to an area where you have never lived, stress your serious desire to relocate. If practical, include on your resume a phone number in your target city where messages may be taken for you. Family members or friends in the area who may house you temporarily may be willing to offer their numbers as a contact for you.

Make long-distance contacts by phone and email. A phone conversation is the next-best thing to a personal interview and can increase your chances of being invited for one. Email can help you keep your phone costs down but may not be as effective as a person-to-person telephone interaction. Be sure to be prepared for a telephone interaction and plan your email messages thoughtfully.

Tell everyone you know that you want to relocate. You may find contacts from surprising sources. If you wish to relocate because of a spouse or partner's plans, his or her employer or graduate school may be able to give you leads or suggestions. It is appropriate for your partner to inquire about whether such help is available. Be aware, however, that many employers and schools are more willing to extend themselves for married couples than for unmarried ones.

Some of the special issues that come up around a long-distance search are challenges in interviewing. Some employers screen distant applicants by telephone, talking with the applicant individually or on a conference call with several decision-makers (see Chapter 4). Others may have video conferencing equipment and ask you to locate equipment in your area so you have a long-distance interactive on-camera interview. Some employers, primarily large organizations or those in urgent need of nursing professionals or for someone with your specialized experience or education, will cover the costs for you to interview on site. At other times and for other employers, this is not possible. The employer will make the offer to cover your interview expenses; if not offered, you may ask if the organization is in a position to cover your travel costs, but don't expect it. The best approach is to arrange for interviews when you are visiting the distant city looking for housing or making a visit.

It may feel risky to make a decision to move before you have a job, but is often a good option in the long run, particularly if you are willing to do temporary work to pay the bills until you find a permanent position. Living in an area you like usually turns out to be worth the effort you spent to make it possible to do so.

Use Electronic Resources

Electronic communications offer nursing professionals cutting-edge opportunities on many levels. In a job search, the quick and easy access to information simplifies fact gathering, offers interchange with others, facilitates a quick transfer of information and allows job openings to reach a wide audience. In spite of the fact that most professional job seekers find that networking person-to-person is the most effective job search strategy, electronic resources are growing in importance. The possibilities for convenient access to information should not be overlooked or underestimated. For a start in learning about how to use online resources, check NetMedEd (www.netmeded.com), a web tutorial designed with health professionals in mind. Use your email account, join list-servs in your discipline or areas of interest, and learn to perform organizational and job-listing research on the World Wide Web. Good comprehensive web job search guides are available in written and electronic form, including, respectively, *Teach Yourself Today: E-Job Hunting* (Indianapolis, Ind.: SAMS Publishing, 2000) by Schlesinger and Musich, and The Riley Guide: Employment Opportunities and Job Resources, a web site by Margaret Riley at www.dbm.com/jobguide/. For more information about using Internet resources, look for *Internet Resource Guide for Nurses and Health Care Professionals* by Mascare, Czar, and Heda (Menlo Park, Calif.; Addison-Wesley, 1999). Also see "Electronic Resumes" in Chapter 3.

Find Job Listings on the Web

Specific web sites designed to provide job listings are numerous. A few of them are listed here. In addition to job board types of sites with keyword job searches, hospitals (neuro-www.mgh.harvard.edu/hospitalweb.nclk) and other organizations often list their job openings on their own home pages.

GENERAL JOB SEARCH SITES
Career Mosaic (www.careermosaic.com)
Chronicle of Higher Education (http://chronicle.merit.edu)
Monster (www.monsterboard.com)
The Riley Guide: Employment Opportunities and Job Resources
   (www.dbm.com/jobguide/)
USA Jobs, a U.S. government site for job postings (www.usajobs.opm.gov)

ADDITIONAL SITES SPECIFIC TO NURSING OR HEALTH CARE
Absolutely Health Care (www.healthjobsusa.com)
American Mobile Healthcare: (www.americanmobile.com/)
American Travel Therapist—for PT, OT, PTA, COTA, SLPs—(http://
amt.traveltherapist.com)
Great Nurse (http://GreatNurse.com)
Health Care Recruitment On-line (www.healthcareers-online.com/
Welcome.htm)
Health Career Web (www.healthcareerweb.com)
Hot Nurse Jobs (www.hotnursejobs.com)
International Medical Corps Nursing Jobs (www.imc-la.org/jobs/jobs.
html)
Medical Ad Mart (www.medical-admart.com)
Medical Matrix (www.medmatrix.org/index.asp)
Medical/Nursing site (www.wwnurse.com)
MED OPTIONS USA (www.medoptions.com/)
Medzilla (www.medzilla.com/)
NP Central (www.nurse.net/jobs)
Nurse Options USA (www.springnet.com/top.shtml)
Nursing Graduates (www.graduatenurse.com)
Nursing Net (www.nursingnet.org/ebds.htm)
Nursing Spectrum Career Fitness On Line (www.nursingspectrum.com)
Pharmaceutical and Bid Jobs (www.hirehealth.com)
UK Nursing Vacancies (www.nursingtimes.net/careers/careers-index.
asp)
www.nurseoptions.com
www.rehaboptions.com

Use the Web for Networking

Keep in touch with colleagues, old friends, and mentors quickly and
easily via email. Many schools produce alumni directories with email
addresses of graduates or offer email list-servs for alumni. Some nursing schools or career offices have online job listings or information
in fields of special interest. Professional organizations have web sites
through which you may identify list-servs or newsgroups for sharing
ideas with others. See "Locate Contact Information" above for helpful
web sites.

Attend Employment Fairs

With planning and preparation, an employment fair can be a valuable job search experience. Schools of nursing, health systems, regional organizations and professional associations sometimes sponsor job fairs.

At an employment fair, nursing candidates meet potential employers and are screened, possibly leading to a formal interview and a job offer. The job fair may also offer you good practice in demonstrating, in a a few minutes, how capable, qualified, and enthusiastic you are.

Before You Register or Attend

Determine in advance what organizations will be represented and what kinds of jobs they may have to offer. If they are organizations for which you would like to work or jobs for which you would like to practice your interviewing skills, you may wish to attend the job fair.

Before You Go

Prepare a resume with which you are comfortable and make multiple copies on good bond paper (at least one for each employer at the fair). Some fair organizers collect resumes for absent employers or for resume books.

Prepare a brief professional presentation to use when talking with recruiters. Practice a sixty-second description of your experience, education and goals as an opening statement. (See "Develop a Self-Talk" above.)

Plan answers to the commonly asked interview questions (see Chapter 4). Interviews, if they take place on site, may be very brief. Inquire in advance as to how the fair is set up. Will there be information and quick interactions only, or will actual interviews be arranged at the site?

Research potential employers who will be represented at the fair. Look at organizational web sites or write for literature so that you can speak knowledgeably about employers and be prepared to discuss why you are interested in working with them.

The Day of the Fair

Dress professionally, but wear comfortable shoes since waiting in line may be required. Bring only professional-looking accompaniments like a leather resume holder, pen, notepad, or small neat bag for cash and personal items. Book bags, suitcases, or backpacks are best left at school, in the car, or in a locker. It is not a good idea to bring children or partners, as professional interaction is your goal. Remember that, even while waiting in line, you are visible to potential employers. You have an opportunity to show your positive and enthusiastic style.

Scout around for a registration table so that you have signed in, received a nametag, or otherwise informed organizers that you have arrived. Check for conveniences like refreshments, lounge, writing table, and lavatory. Read registrant materials. Look over an updated list of participants. Establish priorities for meeting employers and visit first the organizations in which you are most strongly interested. Some participating employers leave early.

Keep your eyes open for special opportunities at the fair. Sometimes absent employers leave contact information, organizers may create resume books for distribution, nursing alumni may be present for networking, or specialized or regional job search resources may be displayed. Attend seminars conducted on a variety of job search and career issues. Talk with your fellow job seekers, from whom you can learn a lot. For those who look, there may be hidden opportunities at a job fair.

When possible, take the business cards of employers you meet or those in whom you may be interested. The cards show the complete name, title, and contact information for the representative.

Approach the employer's table with confidence. Shake hands firmly if a hand is extended. Maintain a friendly expression and attitude and introduce yourself. Talk with the potential employer with energy and enthusiasm, using your self-talk or interview preparation (see Chapter 4).

At the end of the day, jot down anything that you would like to remember. You may even wish to make a few notes immediately following an interesting interaction with an employer. A quick note following a meeting may help you to remember key facts. After a day of short meetings, the facts and faces will quickly become a blur. Write a thank-you note or follow-up communication to employers that interest you (see sample follow-up correspondence in Chapter 3). If appropriate, you can include any detail that was especially important to you or unique to your conversation; it is a good time to show your writing skills and your quick professional style of follow-through.

Development and implementation of a job search strategy bring you face to face with employers. Written materials, in the form of well-prepared resumes and cover letters, are the evidence of your education, accomplishments, competence, and professionalism. Although you have planned well for your job search, the materials viewed by potential employers are often their concrete introduction, or first impression, of you. Even if a potential employer already likes you, the written materials will be shared and evaluated by others in the organization. Tie your professional presentation together with excellent written materials.

3
Written Materials Tool Kit

Resumes: What to Include and How

A resume is a summary of your professional and personal experiences
—education, clinical experience, employment, skills, and interests—
designed to introduce you to potential employers and interest them in
interviewing you. Often your resume is the employer's first impression
of you; don't underestimate its importance.

In order for a resume to be effective, it must be targeted to the employers who are going to read it. A single "catch-all" resume that you
use in looking for various types of jobs is much less effective than several well-focused resumes that highlight pertinent elements in your experience. If you plan to apply for both hospital-based and community-
based positions, for example, you might be better served by having
two resumes, one emphasizing your hospital experience, and the other
highlighting your community health background. Remember, the purpose of a resume is to obtain an interview, so it must convince the
reader that you have something to offer.

Your resume should be no more than two pages, and many professionals feel a one-page resume is best. Often with good editing it is
possible to create a well-focused, powerful, one-page resume. Recent
graduates of baccalaureate nursing programs should use a one-page
resume. A general rule of thumb is to identify only the most pertinent
information and to organize your information in the most concise way
possible. If that requires more than one page, use the additional page.
The only advantage to using two pages is being able to include essential information that would otherwise be lost. Nurses with advanced
degrees will most likely need two pages. If you have a two-page resume,
be sure to put your name at the top of the second page.

Preparation

Before sitting down to write your resume, review your educational, professional and personal history. Make lists of all jobs and experiences (paid and volunteer), schools attended, clubs joined, honors received, skills acquired, duties performed, and any related additional information. These lists will form the basis of your resume and will help you identify your accomplishments. Keep in mind that, unlike a job application given to you by an employer, your resume does not need to include every single thing that you have done. You should include all goal-related experience and account for your time since program completion. You must make choices about what to include or exclude. Also during your preparation, think through the particular skills you would like to emphasize to the employer. For example, if you would like to stress your physical assessment abilities, specify accomplishments demonstrating those abilities.

Basic Content

Your resume should include your name, current and/or permanent address, telephone number, email address, education, honors and awards, and appropriate professional experiences, both paid and unpaid. These are required categories. However, many sections may be added, including but certainly not limited to: job objective, summary of qualifications, clinical rotations/placements, presentations and publications, extracurricular and community activities, certifications, professional memberships, continuing education units, and complementary information like special skills and interests. Throughout your resume, within each section, information should be listed in reverse chronological order, with the most recent item first.

Name, address(es), phone number(s), and email address can be centered on the page or placed in the upper left or upper right. Some advanced degree practitioners add their professional initials (PhD, MSN, PNP, BSN) after their name at the top of the resume, listing their highest-level degrees first. Phone numbers must be included so that potential employers are able to reach you. If there are two phone numbers where you can be reached (home and office) you may include both. An email address demonstrates that you can use technology and facilitates convenient communications. Check your email and voice mail messages regularly to respond to inquiries in a timely manner.

Think carefully about listing both current and permanent addresses. Do you know when you will leave your current address? Will someone at your permanent address take messages? Create a situation in which it is easy for an employer to reach you.

If you plan to relocate, consider adding a contact address or telephone number in the new city. Adding this information sends a clear message that you are firm in your intention to relocate. It also allows a potential employer to reach you or a contact person in the event that their plans change and you are en route to the new city.

Resume Objective

This category (also called professional objective, job objective, career objective) is optional. There may be advantages in using this category because it lets the reader know up front what it is you are looking for. It is particularly useful if you have made a career change and past experience does not reflect your current interests. It is also helpful to have an objective on a resume distributed at job fairs since these are not ordinarily accompanied by a cover letter.

To be most effective, the objective must be specific. An objective such as "pediatric or geriatric nursing position in a large or small hospital" is not specific enough to convince the reader of your commitment to any particular area. You will be better served by an objective such as: "Pediatric nursing position at a university-affiliated hospital." Your objective can also be even more detailed, such as: "Advanced clinical position in the field of women's health care, with opportunity for research." Avoid phrases like "Seek challenging and responsible position" or "Position utilizing my education and skills"; they are overused and tell the reader very little about what you want. It is perfectly appropriate to have several resumes, each with different objectives and/or content to suit particular fields of interest.

If you want to use only one resume for several types of positions, however, you may choose to omit an objective altogether. In this case, you should use your cover letters to target your interest in particular positions.

Qualifications Statement/Profile

This category allows you to summarize the outstanding features of your background that are pertinent to the job(s) you are seeking. A well-written qualifications section can direct the reader to what you want her or him to know and provide clues about what to focus on. Professionals with quite a bit of experience generally use this kind of statement; if you have less experience, your qualifications will be obvious from the descriptions of your previous positions.

As with the job objective, your qualifications statement must make sense to the reader and be as specific as possible. For example, a phrase like, "Outstanding background and clinical training in pediatric, geriatric, and oncology nursing, counseling, management, budgeting, German, and Spanish," even if true, is too complex and difficult for the reader to see its relevance to a specific job.

Good qualifications statements are focused. Two strong examples are as follows: "Experienced critical care practitioner and educator with recent work in long-term management of cardiovascular patients. Additional background in administration and supervision"; "Strong clinical background in individual and family therapy in both inpatient and outpatient settings. Track record as effective leader and consultant. Able to utilize systems approach in problem solving." To prepare an effective qualifications statement you must think carefully about what exactly you can offer an employer.

Summary

A summary is a slightly more in-depth description of experience and history than the qualifications statement or profile. It is designed to orient the reader to your particular qualifications and can sometimes be useful in helping direct a potential employer to see and understand your special strengths and potential contributions. It may also be used to describe special circumstances or to bridge gaps in your work history. It may also refer to work history that complements, but does not directly relate to, health care.

SUMMARY EXAMPLES

Certified Family Nurse Practitioner with prescriptive authority, licensed in NY, NJ, CT, and MA, wishes to work in a collaborative family practice with other Nurse Practitioners. Recent Nurse Practitioner certification and Master's degree complemented by ten years of previous experience as a Registered Nurse.

Registered Nurse with fifteen years of experience in a major medical center seeks to serve in a new setting. Five years of service as a Staff Nurse in med/surg, three years of experience in intensive care and seven years as Nurse Manager of the Outpatient Unit of Paoli Hospital. Prepared to provide effective nursing service in both inpatient and outpatient settings.

Recent BSN/MSN graduate with five years of previous health care experience. Master's coursework and clinicals added to Bachelor's education is preceded by five years of experience in direct patient care as LPN. Attended classes on a part-time basis while working full-time to complete the BSN and MSN programs.

Registered Nurse, currently licensed in TX, TN, AK, and LA with recent coursework at Louisiana State University School of Nursing. Returning to workforce after several years of volunteer hospital service, management of community health fair which included osteoporosis screenings and blood pressure checks, in addition to caring for children. Previous experience includes five years of hospital based staff nursing. Mature, reliable professional, fully prepared to resume full-time hospital-based position.

Education, Awards, Honors, and Campus Leadership

These categories may be combined or separated. What is crucial is that all information be easy to find on the page (see resume samples for different styles of presentation). This section begins with school(s) attended and degree(s) received. When listing dates, it is necessary to list only the date you received (or will receive) your degree, not all the years you attended the school.

If you transferred from another school, it is necessary to list only the school from which you received your degree, unless there is a reason to include the other school (for example, you were very involved in extra-curricular activities and want to include them). Typically, high school is omitted unless there is something meaningful to the reader about the high school that you attended. For instance, if you are applying to positions in religiously affiliated hospitals and you are a graduate of a school with the same affiliation, this is information you may wish to include. If you are a recent graduate of a BSN program or are applying for jobs before graduation and you were a class leader or took on special projects in high school, you may wish to include these special accomplishments.

You may also choose to list the title of your master's thesis (if applicable), research interests, and relevant course work. Often, nurses include senior leadership projects, significant clinical rotations, or practicum experiences in this section, but the information may also be presented in more detail in a separate "Clinical Experience" section. Some students take specialized clinical courses, such as one in IV insertion, and may wish to list certificates acquired. It may be significant for an employer to know this. Experienced professionals may wish to indicate updating of certifications, recent coursework, or skill enhancement seminars in their area of specialization.

In each section, begin with your most recent involvement and list entries in reverse chronological order, working your way back in time. For both activities and honors, you may wish to list entries as subheadings of the college or university where you participated in the activities or earned the honors. If there is reason to highlight them in a separate section, be certain that, in addition to being clearly organized, the information is strong enough to stand on its own.

Even if you were very active in college and can write paragraphs about your extracurricular activities and campus leadership, you should concentrate on selecting only the most interesting or impressive ones. For example, being president of your student government during your junior year would tell an employer about your leadership qualities, but you might leave out that you were on the hospitality committee during freshman year.

Widely known honors (such as Sigma Theta Tau or Phi Beta Kappa) need no explanation, but lesser or local awards can be explained briefly, for example, "Eta Pi Upsilon, Women's Honorary Society." Be sure to include scholarships, fellowships, grants, special awards, and recognition. If the list becomes long and complicated, select the most significant; for example, choose the most well-understood academic, campus leadership, and athletic awards to assist the reader in understanding your strong commitments and success in these areas.

Experience

Of the many approaches you can take to present your experience, the two most common are chronological and functional. A chronological resume is organized around the dates of your experiences, starting with most recent. A functional resume, or skill-based resume, involves an arrangement of your experience around functions you have performed and skills you have developed (see sample resume 7). The most common form of resume is chronological; it has the advantages of being easy to read and more familiar to employers.

The approach you take to listing your experiences on a chronological resume will depend on what you are looking for and what you have done. The only criteria are that you are consistent and clear. In some cases, one general heading titled "Nursing Experience" will be appropriate. In other cases, breaking down your experience into subsections will be most effective. For example; if you are seeking a clinical nurse specialist position and have both clinical and research experience, two separate headings—one "Clinical Experience" and one "Research Experience"—might have more impact than a single "Experience" heading. You may also rearrange the categories according to the job for which you are applying; bring the research experience closer to the top of the resume—where the most pertinent information should be—when applying for a position in research.

Alternatively, you may wish to separate related and unrelated experience, with sections headed "Nursing Experience" or "Clinical Rotations" for nursing-related experience and sections entitled "Employment" or "Additional Work Experience" for unrelated positions. Each category should list your most recent experience first. It is perfectly appropriate to include unpaid work in your experience section. However, it is important that you make the reader aware of which were paid and which were volunteer positions.

Your approach will be somewhat different for the functional resume (sample resume 7). You may want to organize your experiences around roles you've filled or skills you possess, particularly if you are looking for a position that is not related to your previous specific job titles. The emphasis will fall on what you have done, not on where you worked or your job classification. For example, if you are seeking a mid-level administrative nursing position, you might want to list and describe your management, programming, supervisory, teaching, and clinical skills separately from the positions in which you actually used them. Since most employers want to know your job titles and employer names, functional resumes may not be as well received as chronological. In order to get the best of both types of resume, create another section in the functional resume that lists position titles, along with employer names and dates of service, without descriptive passages. The skill-based information early in the resume will get the focus of attention, deemphasizing your current job title.

Try to describe your experience in an interesting way, while being as brief as possible. Don't feel you need to sacrifice clarifying details about important accomplishments, though, for the sake of brevity. The use of action verbs to describe what you did (see the action verb list) will make you seem direct and action-oriented. Ask yourself the question "What did I do?" to identify action verbs that will effectively describe your job responsibilities.

Phrases like "Responsibilities included (or duties included) assessing patients' needs upon registration" can be phrased more persuasively (and simply) by saying, "Assessed patient acuity at intake." Descriptions need not be phrased in full sentences. Ask yourself the question "So what?" to determine which aspects of your past are important enough to include on your resume. The question in the employer's mind is "Why should I speak with this person? Why are they different than other nurses I've heard from?" Try to answer that question in your description.

While in the preparation stage it is vital to brainstorm everything about your background; it is equally important to weed out unnecessary information and highlight what is relevant. For example, if you've been an administrator for the past five years, a staff nurse for ten years before that, and are looking for an administrative position, you may not want to include every single staff nurse position you ever held. You can however, find creative ways to summarize years of experience and take up a minimal amount of space. In general, give more detailed accounts about the most recent five years and summarize versions of experiences prior to that. If you worked for the same employer for many years but in various positions, you may wish to name the employer, listing the most high-level job title you earned and adding in parentheses beside the title "(various job titles with steadily increasing levels of responsibility)."

Identify your accomplishments, achievements, and successes in each of your positions and as a whole. Did you chair a fund-raising drive that raised more money than any year in the past? Were you invited by the director of medicine to join a hospital-wide task force? Did you develop materials on a health care issue that have been adopted by the clinic in which you worked? If so, be specific about these achievements on the resume. Even if the job you held is not directly relevant to your job objective, it is likely that you learned skills such as organizing, negotiating, or managing time effectively that are relevant to the job you seek.

Describe your current work setting when moving to another area. You may wish to provide a description of the workplace following the name of your employer. It is sometimes helpful to describe the type of facility in which you worked. You may also wish to say what types of patients you served and how many: "West Texas branch of the Southwestern Medical Center serving community needs from short-term psychiatry to air-evacuated trauma patients"; "Sixty-bed unit serving Orthopedic, Gynecology and trauma patients."

USEFUL ACTION VERBS FOR RESUMES

addressed	calculated	coordinated
administered	catalogued	corresponded
advised	chaired	counseled
alleviated	coached	created
amplified	collaborated	decreased
analyzed	collected	delegated
anticipated	combined	demonstrated
arranged	communicated	designed
assessed	complied	determined
assisted	computed	developed
assumed	condensed	devised
authorized	conducted	devoted
bargained	constructed	diagnosed
broadened	contacted	diagrammed
budgeted	contributed	directed

displayed	managed	reduced
distributed	measured	referred
drafted	mediated	regulated
edited	mentored	rehabilitated
elected	modified	reinforced
eliminated	monitored	related
established	negotiated	reorganized
estimated	observed	replaced
evaluated	operated	represented
examined	orchestrated	reproduced
exhibited	ordered	researched
experimented	organized	reshaped
explained	oriented	resolved
explored	overhauled	restored
facilitated	oversaw	revamped
guided	participated	reviewed
implemented	performed	revised
incorporated	planned	satisfied
increased	predicted	scheduled
influenced	prepared	selected
initiated	prescribed	sold
innovated	presented	solved
inspected	printed	supervised
installed	processed	sustained
instituted	programmed	taught
interpreted	promoted	trained
interviewed	provided	translated
introduced	raised	treated
investigated	recognized	updated
led	recommended	used
lowered	recorded	won
maintained	recruited	wrote

Licenses and Certifications

These may be listed as a separate category following your experience or may follow the "Education" section. They can also be in your "Education" section under a subheading. It should be clear to the reader in what state and field you are licensed or certified. When listing your licenses, do not give your license numbers. It is sufficient to say "Registered Nurse: Pennsylvania and New Jersey."

Community Service or Community Leadership

Employers are frequently interested in knowing what you have done in addition to your work experiences, or how you have become involved as a citizen. Commitments such as volunteer work with Big Brothers/Big Sisters, charity or youth organizations, or alumni associations can help to make you stand out.

Publications and Presentations

Publications and presentations may be one section or two, depending on the quantity of material you have. They should be listed in standard bibliographic form for your field. If you have many entries in these areas and are applying for teaching positions in academic institutions, you will probably need to write a curriculum vitae or c.v. (See the section below on writing a c.v.) Many nursing graduates have not yet acquired a list of publications and presentations, so do not feel that something is missing if you have yet to contribute in this way.

In applying for clinical positions it may be wise to determine an employer's receptivity to your work outside direct clinical practice before you present these accomplishments. You may wish to list publications and presentations on a separate page and present the information in an interview only if it seems appropriate. You may wish to include them in the original body of the resume if the papers or presentations are related to the specific field in which you are seeking a job.

Professional Memberships

Just as community leadership shows that you are a good public citizen, listing professional memberships shows that you are an active professional citizen. In every profession there are relevant associations that give members a chance to interact with each other and keep up with current developments in the field. It is highly advisable that you join at least one professional association (see Appendix 3). If you have been active in any professional organization, (held leadership roles or participated in important committees) you might benefit by mentioning not only the organization but also your level of involvement, either on your resume or in your cover letter.

Additional Information: Background, Special Skills, and Interests

This is the place to put interesting miscellaneous information that employers may find intriguing but that does not fit anywhere else. Some examples are special skills (such as computer expertise, fund-raising); certifications outside the field of nursing; foreign or computer languages known; travel or living abroad; arts, music, or sports background; and personal interests.

Be specific about your interests. A description such as: "Enjoy multicultural communications through travel to Spanish-speaking countries; climb high-altitude mountains; read detective stories," is a lot more interesting than "Interests include travel to South America, mountain climbing, and reading."

Please note that this section is optional and is generally most useful if you have limited experience and therefore want to give an employer a better idea of who you are as a person. If the body of your resume has included the things you think are important, and you feel that an "additional information" section is not relevant, it isn't necessary to include it.

Omit personal information such as date of birth, marital status, parenting experience, Social Security number, height, and weight. This information does not reflect on your ability to perform the job for which you are being considered. It is inappropriate and probably illegal for employers to ask about any of this except your Social Security number. An exception may be in fields like midwifery or pediatrics, where having your own children or staying at home to raise children could be an asset to your candidacy in the field.

References

There is no reason to list references on the resume. In fact, you may want to pick and choose which references to send to any particular job. It is sufficient to state "References available upon request." Some people consider it appropriate to omit this statement altogether as it is obvious that employers can obtain your references by requesting them from you. If however, you have referees who are so distinguished that inclusion of their names adds to your qualifications, then list them individually on a separate sheet of matching paper.

Most universities provide a reference or credentials service for students who would like to store their letters of reference in one place. Check with your school, probably in the career services area, to see how to have your letters stored and to learn what procedures are involved in forwarding them to employers.

Resumes for Different Levels of Experience

Recent graduates of nursing programs may wish to include work or school experiences that are not health-related. When seeking your first nursing position, it may be relevant for a nurse recruiter or health care employer to know that you were a leader in high school, won honors for your athletics, or were recognized for leadership in your community. Nurse recruiters or other health care providers who consider you for a summer position or for one of your first nursing jobs seek clues about what they may expect from you. As an underclassman or new graduate with little or no nursing experience, you may also wish to include jobs that are not health-related. A potential employer needs to know that you are reliable and know what it's like to hold a job.

If you have had a professional life in another field, include the experience on your resume. It will not appear first, since the person hiring you is seeking a health care professional and that will be the focus of your resume, but a section entitled "Experience in Advertising" (or Finance or Development) is appropriate and enriches your application as a nurse. The non-health-related experience will follow the health-related experience. If your previous positions were in social services, scientific research, physical therapy or other health-related fields, you may wish to use a category called "Health-Related Experience" following your nursing experience.

Nurses with depth of experience may choose to highlight your greatest strength by describing your nursing experience in the first section of the resume, following a summary of qualifications or objective if these are included. Whereas a recent graduate's most valuable assets may be the BSN or MSN degrees and clinical rotations, the experienced nurse may wish to highlight accomplishments at work.

Nurses returning to the workforce after a pause in career will present information that supports skills cultivated both in and outside nursing. You may be returning to the job force after working at home with children or after teaching science to high school students. Perhaps while out of the workforce you earned respect from other parents for organizing the annual neighborhood health fair, or served as the volunteer school nurse substitute, or earned accolades from parents and administrators as an excellent science teacher. Your resume should cover nursing education and experience and also include the science teaching or health-related community organizing experience. Determine what skills you have developed in your recent experience that relate to your goals as a nurse. If you are current on professional readings and certifications or you have completed recent coursework, be sure to highlight these accomplishments in your resume as well as in the cover letter. Be sure to list coursework that is under way or certifications and licenses for which you have applied. Include any activities that have helped you to stay current in clinical practice or that allowed you to regain practice skills (continuing education programs or "refresher" courses). Maturity and experience outside nursing can add richness to a health care team and even add needed skills.

Nurses who undertake a change of career may place work experience or education that is most relevant to your current goals as the first section of the resume. If, for example, you are seeking a job as a medical editor, your previous editing and writing experience, as well as the nursing education and clinical experience, will be relevant. The writing and editing experience will probably be first on the resume, however, since this is the direction in which you are moving. If you performed duties related to editing while working as a staff nurse, it will be important to mention these accomplishments on the resume. Under a section describing the job as staff nurse, you might describe editing work on the in-house nursing newsletter or list publications to which you contributed. A clear commitment to the new career field should be emphasized in the resume layout, word choices, and in the accompanying materials.

Resume Layout and Appearance

Layout is crucial to the impression your resume makes. Choose a style and stick with it throughout the document. Resumes are skimmed before they are read, so use indentation, capitalization, spacing, boldface, and italics to make it easy for the reader to find the pertinent information. Be sure that the resume is easy to read, however, so be consistent with use of a simple style throughout. In an initial glance at your resume, the important information should stand out. To make for easy reading, leave plenty of white space, using bold type to bring attention to important information on the left side of the page, such as the names of educational institutions and employers. Use a plain type style, like Times New Roman, and the size should be no smaller than nine points. Choose italics sparingly, perhaps to emphasize a single word like "Honors" or for the title of your thesis. Adhere to a consistent pattern with only a few spaces between indentions. A good check for whether or not your resume is effective is to show the resume for five or ten seconds to a friend and then ask them which points they remember, or what items they saw first.

Use the samples in this book as guides in preparing your resume. Make a draft of one or several resumes, and have other people review them. At most schools, current students and alumni have access to a career counselor who can review resumes. You may also want to show the resume both to a person involved in the particular field to which you are applying and to another person with no connection to the field. A variety of viewpoints will help you make more informed choices. If you would like to see additional resume styles, school career offices often have resume books or resume models to review.

Although it is important to include dates in each section (i.e., when you received degrees, worked at particular jobs), they do not need to be prominent. This could mean including them on the right rather than the left side of the resume or incorporating them into position descriptions.

Print your resume on good quality heavy bond paper. Your resume will form the first impression someone has of you, so appearance matters. When printing your resume choose white or off-white bond paper at stationery or printing shops. Photocopy paper is not good quality paper. Cover letters and envelopes should be on matching bond paper. Use a laser printer, not a dot matrix. Use two sheets of paper for two-page resumes; don't copy front and back on one sheet. Folding the resume and cover letter in a standard business envelope is the norm.

Curriculum Vitae or Resume?

Occasionally you may be asked to submit a c.v. or vita. What is being requested is essentially a more detailed resume. Generally, c.v.s are required only for upper-level administrative or college or university teaching positions. Sometimes an ad or employer will ask for a c.v. when they really require only a resume. Your c.v. might elaborate on course work, research, papers written, positions held, courses you are prepared to teach, and research interests. For more detailed information about preparing a c.v., see *The Academic Job Search Handbook*, third edition, by Mary Morris Heiberger and Julia Miller Vick (Philadelphia: University of Pennsylvania Press, 2001).

Electronic Resumes

In today's job market, applicants should be ready to draft documents that can be read by a variety of digital systems. Be prepared to submit resumes for emailing, scanning, and keyword searching.

Here are some tips for email and "cut and paste" submissions. Some organizations encourage delivery of resumes as email, and others encourage cutting and pasting of a resume into a designated space on their home page. Whenever possible, include a cover letter with your resume. Email and "cut and paste" are relatively simple procedures that should be part of your job searching tool kit. If you are unfamiliar with email and the Internet, you should get some basic instruction and become familiar with Web exploration. Internet Medical Education (www.netmeded.com) offers a tutorial in net usage designed for health care professionals.

Although it may be simple to email or to send your resume and cover letter as an email attachment, employers have varying needs and preferences. First, when you can, check with the potential employer before you use attachments. Large corporate employers often prefer attachments, yet some employers are loathe to open documents that could contain viruses or may be unable to access your attachment due to equipment differences. It is possible that you will send an attachment that is never opened. If you determine that attachments are not the best choice for a particular employer, you can be aware of some safeguards to give greater effect or enhance the appearance of your documents.

When it is a better choice to submit the resume as a straightforward email message, use the ASCII format by saving your resume as a text file in a word-processing program. Almost any program or system can interpret ASCII format.

To preserve the appearance of your email resume and cover letter, it is a good idea to limit each line of text to 60 to 72 characters. Text on a longer line will roll over to the line below, rearranging the layout that you originally created. You may wish to email your final resume draft to yourself so that you can see, firsthand, how it appears.

There are special rules for preparing a scannable resume. Employers who place resumes in large electronic databases and search for specific elements in candidates' resumes may require a scannable resume; when they require it, they will request it. Very large corporate employers, like pharmaceutical companies, are most likely to ask for the scannable type. Results are best with a simple resume saved as text-only in ASCII and formatted in a plain 10 to 12 point font. Use white paper, black ink, and a good quality printer, not a dot matrix printer or fax. Avoid italics, boldface, underlining, shading, and graphics as well as the use of tabs. Use the asterisk symbol in lieu of the bullet. Don't fold or staple a resume that may be scanned. Clarity in the quality of your scannable resume, and the precision with which the scanner can interpret its text, depend on following these guidelines. A fold, for example, may obscure the text. In lieu of italics and bold type, use capital letters for section headings and important words. If you have many years of experience and must use a two-page resume, be certain that your name is on the second page. When mailing your resume for scanning, enclose it in a large flat envelope with stiff backing, like cardboard.

Keyword Searches

Although employers of nursing professionals rarely use this type of search, it is good to be aware of its existence. Resumes scanned into large databases are sometimes sorted by keywords and, if selected, forwarded electronically to decision-makers.

As in other resume styles, select your words thoughtfully. Compared to the paper version, where action verbs are preferred, a keyword search takes advantage of the use of nouns and skill- and discipline-based language. During a scan, a computer may hone in on keywords specific to a field of interest. Nouns such as nurse manager, quality control supervisor, health care consultant, certified nurse midwife, teacher, or lactation specialist, and keywords and phrases like preventative care, home health care, bilingual, EKG, geriatric, family practice, and occupational health are the appropriate form for scanning. Scanners are often coded to understand abbreviations like RN and MSN. Be certain that you use the common words for the industry in which you wish to work because the computer will search for these specific terms. Choose effective words so that when your resume is viewed electronically, it will be selected for review by the person with hiring authority.

To learn more about preparation and submission of electronic resumes check the web, of course. Begin with sites like: Rebecca Smith's eResumes and Resources (www.eresumes.com/tut_keyres_examples.html); Wall Street Journal Careers (www.careerjournal.com); Resume Writing Tips by Regina Pontow (www.provenresumes.com/reswkshps/electronic/electrespg1.html), Posting Resumes Online (www.computerbits.com).

Send a paper copy and cover letter after an electronic submission unless otherwise indicated by the employer. For employers of special interest to you, send a hard copy of your resume and a focused cover letter at the same time as the electronic version. Do not rely solely on electronic submissions. Although numbers are rising, relatively few people —usually only those in technical fields— reach the interview stage in the job search process solely on the basis of an electronically submitted resume.

Sample Resumes

Sample Resume 1: BSN

BONNY BELL
Email@School.edu

Street Address, Apt. #
City, State Zip
(000)-000-0000

EDUCATION

RUTGERS, The State University of New Jersey, College of Nursing, Newark, NJ
Bachelor of Science in Nursing, Cum Laude, May 2001
Honors and Leadership: Sigma Theta Tau, Dean's List (GPA 3.5), Chairperson of Community Service Group
Certificates: CPR, IV Insertion, ECG, Arterial Blood Gas Analysis, Mechanical Ventilation
Registered Nurse: New Jersey, New York, Pennsylvania

CLINICAL ROTATIONS

ADULT HEALTH, St. Mary's Life Center: Developed protocol for sensory impaired members
COMMUNITY HEALTH, Newark Senior High School: Conducted physical assessments and health screenings
CHILD HEALTH, UMDNJ University Hospital: Developed knowledge of acute and chronic pediatric care issues
FAMILY CARE, UMDNJ University Hospital: Practiced family-centered approach to care of acute and chronic ills

HEALTH-RELATED EXPERIENCE

Hospital of the University of Medicine and Dentistry of New Jersey, Newark, NJ
Trauma and Mental Health Research Assistant, 2000–Present
- Identified and interviewed research subjects; collected, compiled and analyzed data; prepared reports

Calvary Hospital, Bronx, NY
Nurse Extern, Summer, 2000
- Performed routine patient care on a high-risk maternity unit

Hospital for Special Surgery, New York, NY
Nursing Assistant, Summer, 1999
- Assisted with activities of daily living; promoted restoration of independence in Rehabilitation Unit

Rutgers, The State University of New Jersey, Athletic Department Training Center, Newark, NJ
Assistant Trainer Volunteer, 1998–1999
- Assisted therapist in treating athletic injuries

ADDITIONAL WORK EXPERIENCE

Rutgers, The State University of New Jersey, Career Services Department, Newark, NJ
Office Assistant (work study position—contributed twenty hours per week), 1999–2000
- Assisted with organization of job fairs; utilized databases; prepared and distributed information

JP Morgan, New York, NY
Administrative Assistant, Summer 1997
- Assisted analysts with organizational work; interacted effectively with clients

COMMUNITY SERVICE

BIG SISTER: Mentored a third-grade inner-city child; assisted with school assignments; planned outings
HABITAT FOR HUMANITY HOMEBUILDER: Assisted with rebuilding a home for inner-city residents
MULTIDISCIPLINARY COMMUNITY TEAM MEMBER: Served homeless at community health center providing physical assessments, treatment of minor conditions, and referrals to community resources

Sample Resume 2: Recent BSN Graduate

ASHTON WINTERS

School: Address, Phone number
Home: Address, Phone number
Email address

EDUCATION

University of Tennessee, Memphis, TN	May 2002

Bachelor of Science in Nursing
Activities: Varsity Lacrosse, Field Hockey Team
Coordinator of community service project, Nursing Student Rep
to faculty and staff

Arlington Central High School, Arlington, VA   June 1998
Honors & Leadership: Officer in student senate
President of Class, All-Star state lacrosse MVP

CLINICAL ROTATIONS

St. Joseph Hospital, Memphis, TN   2001–2002
Medical / Surgical – Trauma / Orthopedic Floor

St. Francis Hospital, Memphis, TN   Spring 2001
Community Health Outpatient Education Clinic

St. Jude's Children's Research Hospital, Memphis, TN   Fall 2000
Maternal / Child / Neonatal ICU

Baptist Memorial Health System, Memphis, TN   Spring 2000
Psychiatric / Mental Health

HEALTH-RELATED EXPERIENCE

Health Center Intern, Arlington, VA   Summer 2001
The Mann School
   • Assessed severity of student illnesses and injuries

Personal Care Assistant, Alexandria, VA   Summer 2000
Individual Client
   • Assisted client with hygienic needs, feeding, transfers

Health Care Aide, Washington, DC   Summer 1999
Individual Patient
   • Facilitated physical therapy and personal care

COLLEGE COMMUNITY SERVICE

Vice President and Peer Educator: Drug and Alcohol Resource Team
Tutor in Health and Science: Assisted peers in science
Big Brother: buddied with six-year-old inner-city child

Sample Resume 3: Recent BSN Graduate

Geraldine M. Navoy
Current address: School Street Address, City, State Zip (000) 000-0000
Permanent Address: Home Street Address, City, State Zip (000) 000-0000
Email: Email@location.com

EDUCATION

Catholic University of America, School of Nursing   Washington, DC
*   Candidate for Bachelor of Science in Nursing   May 2002
*   Honors: Elected to Sigma Theta Tau, Spring 1999; Dean's List 1998–2000
*   Certified in advanced critical care modules (ECG, ABG, Hemodynamic Monitoring,
    Mechanical Ventilation, Fluid and Electrolyte, IV Insertion)

SIGNIFICANT CLINICAL ROTATIONS

Children's National Medical Center   Washington, DC
*   Senior Leadership: Pediatric Acute Transplant Oncology floor.   Fall 2002
*   Provide care for 2–3 patients under preceptor supervision.

Hospital for Sick Children   Washington, DC
*   Pulmonary Unit and general Medical Surgery Unit.   Spring 2001

Columbia Hospital for Women Medical Center   Washington, DC
*   Labor & Delivery, Neonatal Intensive Care Unit, Post-Partum and   Fall 2001
    Newborn Nursery.

Psychiatric Institute of Washington   Washington, DC
*   Pediatric Psychology Unit.   Spring 2000

OTHER EXPERIENCE

University of North Carolina Hospitals   Chapel Hill, NC
General Medical Surgery Unit, *Nurse Technician*   Summer 2001
*   Pediatrics, orthopedics, oncology. Assist patients with activities of daily living and transfers.
    Collaborate with health care team.

Personal Residence, *Caregiver for Child with Leukemia*   Chapel Hill, NC
*   Assisted with client's activities of daily living   Summer 2000
    Attended to individual needs of client and organized daily schedule.

Catholic University of America   Washington, DC
Admissions Office, *PT Office Assistant* (10 hours per week)   Sept. 1999–May
                                                                           2001

Children's National Medical Center   Washington, DC
Child Life, *Volunteer*   Summer 1999
*   Helped develop physical and mental skills through play. Provided emotional
    support to infants and toddlers who require ventilation and/or rehabilitation.

ACTIVITIES/LEADERSHIP

*   Student Nurses Association: *Delegate*, 2002 State Convention, organized
    career workshops and career fair
*   *Executive Board member*, Kappa Alpha Theta Sorority
*   *Peer Advisor* to transfer students and *Tour Guide*, Undergraduate Admissions
*   *Ambassador* and *Host for Prospective Students*, Catholic Student Organization

SKILLS

*   Proficient in German
*   Familiar with Windows 95/98, Microsoft Word, PowerPoint, Excel and
    Internet Browser Software

Sample Resume 4: BSN with Previous Degrees and Hours for Clinicals

Elaine Stein
Current Address
City, State Zip Code
Phone Number; Email Address

Education

- State University of New York at Binghamton, School of Nursing: BSN, May 2002
- Kenyon College, Gambier, OH: BA, Integrative Biology, May 1999
- Kenyon College, Gambier, OH: BA, Religious Studies, December 1998

Clinical Experience

Senior Leadership Clinical, Cardiac Intensive Care Unit, Our Lady of Lourdes Memorial Hospital, Binghamton, NY (16 hours/week, September 2001-December 2001)
- Worked directly with staff nurse preceptor in patient care planning and implementation
- Participated in family liaison process during patient's operative course
- Developed and refined nursing skills related to care of pediatric cardiac patients

Pediatric and neonatal clinical rotation, Our Lady of Lourdes Memorial Hospital, Binghamton, NY (12 hours/ week, March 2001-May 2001)
Planned and implemented direct patient care on medical-surgical pediatric unit
Implemented patient care under RN supervision in neonatal intensive care unit

Health-Related Experience

Our Lady of Lourdes Memorial Hospital, Binghamton, NY
Research Assistant, Opioids and patient satisfaction of pain management study (June 2001-Present)
- Interview oncology patients in Hematology/Oncology Clinic
- Chart data related to chemotherapy, radiation, and pain medication

Research Assistant, Risk for thromboembolic events related to intravenous gamma globulin and plasmapheresis therapy study (June 2001-Present)
- Analyze data on incidence of stroke, deep vein thromboses, pulmonary emboli, and myocardial infarction
- Collaborate with research team in developing study protocol and correlate thromboembolic events with intravenous gamma globulin or plasmapheresis therapy

Research Assistant, Risks for early failure of arterio-venus fistulas study (May 2001-August 2001)
- Conducted interviews with dialysis patients
- Renewed and recorded data on fistula creation, end-stage renal disease, and renal transplant

Binghamton School of Nursing
Interviewer, Teaching Assistant, Coordinator, Health Service Internship Program (September 1999-May 2000)
- Interviewed and placed interns in public health organizations, community outreach
- Led discussions on public health issues

School Leadership

President, Sub Rosa, Women's Social & Service Group, SUNY-Binghamton (2001–2002)
- Coordinated with group members to organize University and community events
Volunteer, Health Clinic, SUNY-Binghamton (September 2000-May 2001)
- Collaborated efforts with University schools provide free health care and legal services to the local community

Sample Resume 5: BSN Including High School Accomplishments and Study Abroad

VICTORIA MEDLIN   Email@provider.com

School Box #, School Street Address, City, State Zip Code   (000) 000-0000
Home Address, City, State Zip Code   (000)-000-0000

EDUCATION

UNIVERSITY OF VIRGINIA, School of Nursing, Charlottesville, VA
Bachelor of Science of Nursing, Minor in Nutrition (GPA 3.49), degree expected May 2002
 • Primary undergraduate member, *Undergraduate Curriculum Committee*
 • Member, *Student Health Advisory Board*
 • Chair, Special Events, *Phi Sigma Pi*
HENRIETTA SZOLD HADASSAH-HEBREW UNIVERSITY, School of Nursing, Jerusalem, Israel
 • Semester Study and Clinical Nursing Experience abroad. (Spring 2001)
MILTON ACADEMY, Houghton, MA
 • High School Diploma (1998)
 • Editor-in-Chief, *The Scribe,* school newspaper
 • Award winner, *Silver Award* for Excellence & Achievement in Chemistry
 • Nursing observation, Franklin Medical Center, Greenfield, MA

CLINICAL EXPERIENCE

MEDICAL INTENSIVE CARE NURSING, University of Virginia Health Science Center (Spring 2002)
 • Independently oversee patients with minimal supervision by preceptor
 • Provide total nursing and administrative care: ½ to full nurse's load working whole shift
PSYCHOLOGICAL AND COMMUNITY NURSING, University of Virginia Health Science Center
(Fall 2001)
MEDICAL/SURGICAL AND GERONTOLOGICAL NURSING, University of Virginia Health Science
Center (Spring 2001)
 • Delivered all aspects of nursing care for 1–4 patients
 • Directed and followed through on patient care, oversaw medications, led patient
   education and discharge planning
PEDIATRIC, LABOR & DELIVERY, AND POSTPARTUM NURSING, Hadassah Hospital, Jerusalem,
Israel (Fall 2000)
 • Taught baby care to 1–8 patients each week
 • Utilized Hebrew language and other communication techniques
 • Applied cultural sensitivity and recognized cultural values, ideologies, and customs
ONCOLOGY, OBSTETRICAL, AND GENERAL SURGERY OBSERVATION, Franklin Medical Center
(Spring 2000)

HEALTH-RELATED EMPLOYMENT

GROUP EXERCISE INSTRUCTOR, University of Virginia Department of Recreation (Fall
2001-Present)
 • Choreograph and modify cardiovascular and strength training routines
 • Simplify complicated movements for effective training
PRIMARY RESEARCH ASSISTANT, Infant Nutrition & Breastfeeding Services Study, University of
Virginia (1999–2002)
 • Resolved scheduling conflicts among study participants, researchers, and extra-family
   participants
 • Organized large body of data using Excel and Access databases, addressing all details
 • Interviewed subjects, developed calendars, and charted interactions
DATABASE RESEARCHER, University of Virginia (Summer 1999–2002)
 • Researched independently using medical search engines, time management techniques,
   library resources, and effective written communications

CERTIFICATIONS

American Heart Association, Class C Health Care Provider, Adult and Infant CPR and Heimlich
Maneuver
Aerobics and Fitness Association of America, Group Exercise Instructor
International Sports Conditioning Association, Ultimate Frisbee Instructor
Intravenous Insertion, University of Virginia (Spring 2001)
Electrocardiogram Reading, University of Virginia (Spring 2001)

Sample Resume 6: BSN/Recent Graduate/Business (Health Care) Minor at Well-Known Business School

Darren Clark
Email@server.edu/nursing

Permanent Address:	**School Address:**
Street Address	Street Address
City, State Zip Code	City, State Zip Code
Telephone	Telephone

EDUCATION	**University of Texas at Austin,** Austin, TX Bachelor of Science in Nursing, Summa Cum Laude	May 2002
	LBJ School of Business: Minor in Health Care Management	
SIGNIFICANT CLINICALS	**Hospital of the University of Texas,** Austin, TX Medical/Surgical-Cardiology with telemetry, Liver/ Renal transplant Pediatric-Respiratory and Gastroenterology Unit, Cardiac Stepdown Community Health-Outpatient clinic	2000–2002
	Austin State Hospital, Austin, TX Psychiatry-Drug and Alcohol, Long-term Care	1999
WORK EXPERIENCE	**Methodist Health Care Center,** Houston, TX Student Nurse Extern- Cardio-thoracic and General Surgical • Assisted in all aspects of patient care (18 beds) • Obtained vital signs, EKG's, blood glucose, lab samples • Educated and monitored patients one-on-one	Summer 2001
	Twelve Oaks Hospital, Houston TX Nursing Assistant- Medical-Surgical Adult Primary Care • Monitored patient status under supervision of N.P. • Performed complete physical exams, maintained charts • Analyzed patient history to facilitate diagnosis / treatment	Summer 2000
	Institute Mexicano, Mexico City, Mexico Nurse Educator / Nurse Extern • Provided community outreach and immunizations • Reviewed and evaluated patient record keeping	Summer 1999
	Texas School of Business, Austin, TX Research Assistant / Office Assistant • Supported technical systems / sorted records • Managed databases	Spring 1998
AWARDS & LEADERSHIP	Sigma Theta Tau President, Student Nurse Association Greater Houston Achievement Award for Service to others	
SPECIAL SKILLS	Language: Fluent in Spanish Computing: Microsoft Office (Word, PowerPoint, Access, Outlook), ACT, familiar with PC and MAC applications	

Sample Resume 7: Functional Resume for Clinician Seeking a Supervisory/Management Position

Andrea Shilling
Street Address
City, State Zip Code
(000)-000-0000 — Email@abc.com

EXPERIENCE IN MANAGEMENT AND SUPERVISION

Supervision and Evaluation
- Recommended work flow changes which continue to be in use
- Assumed charge nurse responsibilities and served as preceptor for new staff members
- Trained new employees and prepared recommendations for performance evaluations
- Presented a series of in-service training sessions for new nurses

Management and Organization
- Utilized total quality management techniques in training and overseeing new employees
- Initiated support groups for patients and their families
- Managed heavy telephone triage during distant emergencies
- Coordinated follow-up care
- Served on critical-care division quality assurance committees
- Designed and established patient care and tracking method for unit
- Utilized shared governance model while providing patient-centered care

Program Development
- Presented hospital-wide in-service training sessions on elder abuse
- Developed series of workshops for physicians to help identify elder abuse
- Co-chaired unit education committee
- Contributed to suicide risk and assessment program

Financial Management
- Managed budget ($150,000) for volunteer organization with over 1,000 volunteers serving Columbus schools

Training
- Cross-trained candidates for ICU
- Created training materials
- Educated hospital health care providers on the need for documentation of painful episodes in ICU

EMPLOYMENT

Boone Hospital Center, Columbia, Missouri
ICU Nurse, 1997–present

Columbia Regional Hospital, Columbia, Missouri
Staff Nurse, 1993–1997

EDUCATION

University of Missouri—Columbia, School of Nursing, Columbia, Missouri
Bachelor of Science in Nursing, May 1993
Vice President of Senior Class, Sigma Theta Tau, Clinical Teaching Assistant

COMMUNITY SERVICE

Chairperson, Columbus School District Reading Immersion Program, oversees funding and implementation of major project

Sample Resume 8: Blend of Traditional and Functional Resume Styles

Emphasizes analytical/research experience from a staff nurse position. Could be used for a transition to consulting, government, insurance, research, or nursing administration.

JAKE FRANCIS, RN
Street Address
City, State Zip Code
(000)-000-0000 *Email@provider.com

Summary: Assumed leadership among nursing peers; recognized by administration for excellence in administrative innovation; analytical abilities and needs assessment skills acquired through ten years of clinical nursing experience

HIGHLIGHTS OF ANALYTICAL EXPERIENCE and PROFESSIONAL LEADERSHIP

Quality Assurance Representative: Montgomery General Hospital
Designed and coordinated unit-based study for quality assurance program
Acted as liaison between unit and administration
Analyzed data and prepared recommendations for change
Successfully spearheaded implementation of program
Awarded: Employee of the month for innovations in quality of patient care

JCAHO Representative: Montgomery General Hospital
Compiled statistics on documentation of pain by nurses for JCAHO accreditation
Assessed and wrote report on significance of the statistics

RESEARCH EXPERIENCE

Research Assistant/Clinical Coordinator: Rhone Pharmaceuticals
Recruited, selected and obtained consent from subjects for three-year clinical trial
Analyzed chart contents for risk factors
Collected, organized, and evaluated data using Excel
Coordinated the multicenter study to determine efficacy and safety of drug dosages
Monitored pre-op, intra-op, and post-op care of participants
Prepared and edited manuscripts for submission to scientific journals

HEALTH-RELATED WORK HISTORY

Montgomery General Hospital, Olney, MD
Staff Nurse/Charge Nurse, Various Units 1992–present

Rhone Pharmaceuticals, Crystal City, VA
Part-time Research Assistant/Study Coordinator, 1989–1992
(Worked 20 hrs per week while carrying full-time course load)

EDUCATION

Marymount University, Arlington, VA
Bachelor of Science in Nursing, 1992
HONORS AND LEADERSHIP: Sigma Theta Tau,
*Selected as Commencement Speaker
*Faculty Award for Excellent Potential Leadership in Nursing

Sample Resume 9: Experienced Professional with a Specialty

NEVIS BENJAMIN
Street Address
City State and Zip Code
Telephone (000) 000-0000
Email address@email carrier

Professional Experience with Women and Children

Mount Washington Pediatric Hospital, Baltimore, MD (May 2000–present)
Coordinator of Maternal/Child Program–Facilitate policy and staff development; design and implement documentation, teaching tools, and guidelines; direct case management and discharge planning for maternal-child nurses; conduct antepartum, postpartum, neonatal, and pediatric home visits; perform home health assessment, physical examinations, diagnostic procedures, and treatments; evaluate and monitor lab results; instruct patients and families in health promotion and disease prevention; schedule and participate in 24-hour on-call

Mercy Medical Center, Baltimore, MD (June 1998–Jan. 1999)
Staff Nurse (OB-GYN)–Provided primary nursing care and patient education for antepartum, postpartum, neonatal (Mother/Infant Nursing) and gynecological patients with an emphasis on preventive health care; conducted research study on breast self-examination

Good Samaritan Hospital, Baltimore, MD (May 1997–May 1998)
Staff Nurse (Pediatrics-M/S)–Administered primary nursing care and patient education for infants, children, and adult medical-surgical patients

Union Memorial Hospital, Baltimore, MD (June 1996–May 1997)
Staff Nurse (OB-GYN)–Served patients' antepartum, intrapartum, postpartum, newborn, and gynecological needs *while studying for BSN*

Education

University of Maryland, Baltimore, MD (MSN, 2000)
Women's Health Clinical Specialist Program

University of Maryland, Baltimore, MD (1998–1999)
Parent/Child Case Management Graduate Program Coursework

Towson State University, Towson, MD (BSN 1998)

Baltimore County Community College, Baltimore, MD (ASN 1996)

Nurse Practitioner Clinicals in Women's Health

Planned Parenthood, Baltimore, MD (Jan.–May 2000)
Managed gynecological patients; provided pregnancy dating and prenatal referrals; performed histories and physicals, pelvic and breast examinations, pap smears and diagnostic and treatment procedures; dispensed medications; ordered and evaluated diagnostic tests, provided health education, counseling, referrals, and follow-up care for women of all ages

Nevis Benjamin, page 2

Bexar County OB/GYN Associates, Towson, MD (Sept.–Dec. 1999)
Served gynecological and obstetrical patients; performed admission histories and physical examinations, pelvic and breast examinations, pap smears, diagnostic tests, and health screenings; ordered and evaluated diagnostic studies, wrote prescriptions for medications; provided ongoing care to prenatal and infertility patients; performed endometrial biopsies and IUD insertions, diaphragm and pessary sizing and checks; provided ongoing management through health education, counseling, referrals, and follow-up care to adolescents, childbearing women, peri- and postmenopausal women and for all women with gynecological and general health problems

Franklin Square Hospital, Baltimore, MD (May 1999)
Performed health histories, physical and breast examinations in Surgical Department on women of all ages; evaluated screening and diagnostic procedures; provided health education, counseling, and follow-up care related to breast health

Johns Hopkins Bayview Medical Center, Baltimore, MD (May 1999)
Interviewed patients for histories and physically assessed via pelvic and breast examinations, diagnostic and screening procedures; evaluated pelvic floor dysfunction; administered care for women with vulvodynia, interstitial cystitis, urge and stress incontinence and the sequelae of these conditions; utilized biofeedback, bladder instillations, manual physical therapy, and Interstim (continence control therapy) to manage pelvic floor dysfunction patients

Certifications
  •   Certified Registered Nurse Practitioner (CRNP)
  •   Perivascular Nurse Consultants, Inc., IV Certification
  •   American Heart Association CPR, BLS Certification
  •   Sexual Assault Nurse Examiner (SANE)

Professional Organizations
  •   Sigma Theta Tau International Honor Society of Nursing
  •   Association of Women's Health, Obstetrics, and Neonatal Nurses

Licensure
  •   Maryland, Virginia, and District of Columbia: Registered Nurse (RN)

Sample Resume 10: MSN/NP/Oncology

ALESANDRA GALGON

Street Address
City, State Zip Code
000-000-0000
E-Mail@server.edu

EDUCATION

Auburn University at Montgomery, Montgomery, Alabama
Post Master's Oncology Nurse Practitioner Program, 2002
Master of Science in Nursing, Adult Oncology Program, 2000

Buenos Aires University, Buenos Aires, Argentina
Bachelor of Science in Nursing, 1986

SCHOLARSHIPS AND HONORS

- Award of special recognition, School of Nursing, Auburn University at Montgomery, 1999
- Employee of the year award, Santa Fe del Rio Hospital, Santa Fe, Argentina
- Recipient of scholarships: Oncology Nursing Society, International Union Against Cancer, Rotary International Foundation, Fulbright Commission on the Argentinean government

CLINICAL INTERNSHIPS

Jackson Hospital and Clinic, Montgomery, Alabama
Oncology Nurse Practitioner Student, Hematology Oncology Clinic   January 2002–June 2002
Managed care of cancer patients in both inpatient and outpatient settings in collaboration with oncologist; completed histories and physicals; provided diagnostic, pharmacological, and psychosocial aspects of care

Veterans Administration Medical Center, Montgomery, Alabama
Oncology Nurse Practitioner Student, Pigmented Lesion Clinic   September–December 2001
Oversaw care of patients with malignant melanoma and dysphasic nevi in outpatient setting in coordination with dermatologist/oncologist; prepared histories, performed complete skin examinations; diagnosed, coordinated care, and educated both new and established patients

Oncology Nurse Practitioner Student, Hypertension Clinic   September–December 2001
Managed care of patients with hypertension; performed complete histories and physicals; provided diagnostic, pharmacological, psychosocial, and educational aspects of care

Oncology Nurse Practitioner Student, Cancer Center   September 2000–June 2001
Cared for breast cancer patients in outpatient setting in collaboration with oncologist; provided direct care, coordinated chemotherapy administration, psychosocial care, and patient education

PROFESSIONAL NURSING EXPERIENCE

In the United States

Baptist Medical Center, Montgomery, Alabama
Oncology Advanced Clinical Nurse, Cancer Center   April–October 1999
Collaborated with oncologist in care of adult cancer patients in outpatient setting; performed complete histories and physicals; delivered symptom management, psychosocial care, and patient education; coordinated chemotherapy administration and other health care services

Alesandra Galgon, page 2

Auburn University Hospital, Montgomery, Alabama
Research Coordinator, Colposcopy Clinic   December 1998–April 1999
Coordinated the care of patients utilizing the Colposcopy Clinic; functioned as researcher in
cancer prevention and contributed to GYN-Oncology studies; coordinated care of chemotherapy
patients

Pan American Health Organization, Washington DC
Temporary Consultant on Palliative Care   December 1998

In Argentina

Ministry of Health of Argentina, Valparaiso, Argentina   June 1996–December 1998
Specialist Professional, Chronic Diseases Program
Developed proposal for the National Cancer Control Program

Argentine League Against Cancer, Valparaiso, Argentina
Argentinean Coordinator of the Cancer Prevention Program for Latin America   April 1995–June 1996
Organized and implemented a cancer prevention program

Facilitator, Emotional Support Group for Breast Cancer Patients   January 1994–May 1996

Independent Work, Valparaiso, Argentina
Home Care Nurse   October 1991–January 1994
Provided home care to cancer patients including chemotherapy, symptom management,
psychosocial care, and patient education

Santa Fe del Rio Hospital, Santa Fe Argentina
Oncology Care Coordinator   July 1986–October 1991

RESEARCH ACTIVITIES

Auburn University, Division of Gynecologic Oncology, Montgomery, Alabama
Principal Investigator, Proposal for research project on cancer prevention in minority
populations, 2001

Auburn University, School of Nursing, Montgomery, Alabama
Research Assistant, "Nursing's Impact on Quality of Life Post Prostatectomy," 2000
Research Assistant, "Impact of Informational Audiotapes in Radiation Therapy," 1999
Research Assistant, "Natural Killer Cells over Time in Patients with Colorectal Cancer," 1998

PROFESSIONAL LEADERSHIP

Board of Directors, International Society of Nurses in Cancer Care
Active Member, Oncology Nursing Society
Board Member, Argentinean Association of Oncology Nurses–AAON

LANGUAGES

First Language: Spanish
Second Language: English

Sample Resume 11: Clinical Nurse Specialist/Information Technology

MAYA BOWER

Street Address   000-000-0000
City, State Zip   E-Mail

EXPERIENCE

Columbia Presbyterian Medical Center   New York, NY
CLINICAL INFORMATION TECHNOLOGY SPECIALIST   9/99-Present

- Evaluate, recommend, and implement systems throughout Center
- Train all levels of users in protocols to facilitate technology competency
- Implement technology procedures and guidelines for health care users
- Develop, design, and assess educational programs for health professionals
- Evaluate system validity, reliability, and effectiveness and prepare recommendations
- Assess health system technology needs on ongoing basis and negotiate purchases
- Identify challenges that may be addressed through technological innovation

ICU STAFF NURSE   9/97–9/99

- Oversaw cardiac ICU unit; functioned as charge nurse
- Clinically assessed critically ill surgical patients and executed care plans
- Mentored and evaluated staff and nursing students

Hunter-Bellevue School of Nursing   New York, NY
TECHNOLOGY INSTRUCTOR   1/98–1/2000

- Taught system usage to medical professionals
- Created curriculum for clinical application of technology systems

New York University Medical Center   New York, NY
SENIOR STAFF NURSE   9/95–9/97
- Coordinated clinical services for critical needs patients
- Acted as member of interdisciplinary clinical team
- Contributed to system-wide efficiency as critical issues committee member

EDUCATION

Hunter College of the City University of New York, Hunter-Bellevue   New York, NY
School of Nursing
Master's of Science in Nursing   August 2000
Minor in Health Care Management, Columbia Graduate School of Business

Coursework: Information Systems, Epidemiology, Managed Care, Health Care Marketing,
Applied Financial Management, Operations and Management Science, Health Technology,
Organizational Consulting, Risk Management, Negotiations

Bachelor of Science in Nursing, Cum Laude   May 1995
Sigma Theta Tau, Hunter College Nurse Scholar

MAYA BOWER
Page 2

RESEARCH

Hunter College of the City University of New York, Hunter-Bellevue   New York, NY
School of Nursing
RESEARCH ASSISTANT   1/93–6/94

- Initiated contact with research subjects and generated participant data
- Analyzed data and prepared reports of findings

LICENSURE AND CERTIFICATION AND PROFESSIONAL MEMBERSHIPS

- Licensed as Registered Nurse in New York
- Certified as Critical Care Registered Nurse
- Certified in Advanced Cardiac Life Support
- Member of American Association of Critical Care Nurses
- Selected for membership in Sigma Theta Tau: International Nursing Honor Society

PUBLICATION

M. Bower (1998). "Embracing Information Technology in Medical Settings," *Technology Today* (April 1998), pp. 7–9.

Sample Resume 12: Emphasis on Business Coursework and Projects Based on Clinical/Scientific Experience and Background.

Moving toward business, consulting, or health care administration

ALLISON LAMENT
Street Address
Email address
(000)-000-0000

EDUCATION

University of Pennsylvania, Philadelphia, PA
Master of Science in Nursing and Health Care Administration, December 2002
Academic Honors: *Fellowship Recipient*, GPA 3.95

The Wharton School, University of Pennsylvania, Philadelphia, PA
Minor in Business Administration

Significant Wharton Coursework: Managerial Accounting, Managerial Economics, Corporate Health care Finance, Management & Economics of Pharmaceutical/Biotech and Medical Device Companies, Health Care Marketing, Health Care Management Science, Negotiations

Health care Consulting Projects:
• Contributed to development of business plan for start-up e-commerce/health care company
• Prepared process analysis for Hospital of the University of Pennsylvania nursing service reduction in force; as a result of analysis, several recommendations were implemented

University of Medicine and Dentistry of New Jersey, Newark, NJ
Bachelor of Science in Nursing, May 2000
Honors and Leadership: Board of Directors, League of Women Voters, Sigma Theta Tau, GPA 3.75, Magna Cum Laude

Haverford College, Haverford, PA
Bachelor of Arts in Biology, June 1995
Research Awards: Scientific Research Award, Pew Grant Recipient

CLINICAL AND RESEARCH EXPERIENCE

Hospital of the University of Medicine and Dentistry of New Jersey, Newark, NJ
Critical Care Staff Nurse/Charge Nurse—Level 1 Trauma Unit, June 2000–Present

Allison Lament, page 2

Rehabilitation Consultants, Inc., Moorestown, NJ
Physical Therapy Technician/Administrative Assistant, 1996–2000

Dupont Merck Pharmaceuticals, Glenolden, PA
Research Technician–Pre-clinical animal studies with HIV protease inhibitors, 1995

Hospital of the University of Medicine and Dentistry of New Jersey, Newark, NJ
Volunteer Hospital Aide–Emergency and Physical Therapy Departments, 1993–1994

Thomas Jefferson University, Philadelphia, PA
Research Technician/Recipient of Grant from the Pew Charitable Trusts for Molecular,
Biochemical and Histological research, 1990–1993

PUBLICATIONS

A. Lament (2002). "Loyalty to the Nurse Manager as a Proxy for Organizational Loyalty," *Nursing Management* (manuscript in preparation).

R. E. Anes, A. Lament, H. Quan. "Cetyltrimethylammonium Bromide Discontinuous Gel Electrophoreses: Mr-Based Separation of Proteins and Retention of Enzymatic Activity," *Annals of Biochemistry* (June 1995), pp. 16–18.

PRESENTATION

"Considerations in Choices of Methods for Students in Biochemical Research." Pre-Conference Workshop for Faculty Before Addressing Larger Issues Around Student Research Methods, 45th Annual Conference of Students Research Issues in Biochemistry, November 1995.

References Available Upon Request

Sample Resume 13: Health Care Executive

Jeanette Cole

	Address	
Phone number (Office)	Email Address	Phone number (Home)

QUALIFICATIONS

A health care executive with extensive leadership experience in quality management, cost reduction, change management, infomatics, and customer service. An innovative and results-oriented leader with proven ability in developing successful programs.

EXPERIENCE

TRINITY HOSPITAL, CHICAGO, IL   1999–2001
Vice President
Reported to the President with full P&L responsibility for the administrative and clinical aspects of the Maternal and Children's program. Managed a budget of $5.2 million and a staff of 260.

Selected Accomplishments:
- Achieved 95% Patient Satisfaction rating on Gallup Survey with scores significantly above the comparison group.
- Negotiated contract for neonatology services with reduced costs by 10% and saved $40,000/year.
- Restructured management team for improved operational effectiveness, saving $147,000/year.
- Developed pediatric day hospital program with projected revenues of $150,000.
- Analyzed and implemented a revised pricing structure while simultaneously expanding antenatal testing, increasing net revenue to $180,000.
- Negotiated perinatology contract reducing costs by 25%.
- Developed a Neonatal Nurse Practitioner program which ensured 24-hour coverage.
- Integrated on-site patient registration, reducing processing time by 33%.
- Reduced cost of unit service by 10%.
- Coordinated quality team efforts which reduced the c-section rate. Organized staffing system leading to the classification as "Best Performer."

ADVOCATE HEALTHCARE, CHICAGO, IL   1995–1999
Assistant Vice President
Reported to the Vice President, Patient Care Services, with full responsibility for the Maternal, Pediatric, and Medical-Surgical units as well as the Women's Center. Managed an operating budget of $13.4 million and a staff of 430.

Selected Accomplishments:
- Planned and implemented consolidation and reorganization of services at time of merger.
- Developed and implemented a transition management education training program for the executive team and over 100 management personnel.
- Restructured management saving $120,000/year.
- Implemented capitated radiology agreement and expanded antenatal testing in Women's Center.
- Developed OB/Gyn Residency program resulting in full AOA approval.
- Negotiated collective bargaining agreement with RN union.
- Implemented HDS clinical information system within areas of responsibility.
- Developed regional pediatric plan as member of planning committee.

Jeanette Cole, page 2

UNIVERSITY OF CHICAGO HOSPITAL, CHICAGO, IL   1982–1995
Assistant Director of Nursing (7 years)
Reported to the Vice President of Patient Care Services with responsibility for nine
medical-surgical units. Managed a $12.4 million budget and a staff of 390.

Selected Accomplishments:
- Developed, planned, and implemented quality management program for nursing
  department resulting in a score of 1 from JCAHO.
- Implemented an automated medication documentation system (PDM) with direct
  order entry.
- Implemented nursing management software program and scheduling system (ANSOS).
- Revised the documentation system for nursing department.
- Selected as the only clinical representative on the team which developed a strategic plan
  for automation of information needs in several divisions.
- Implemented professional development program for new nurse managers on fiscal
  management, performance evaluation, interviewing, CQI, and models of care delivery.

Critical Care Nursing Supervisor (3 years)
Nursing Supervisor (3 years)

NORTH PARK COLLEGE, CHICAGO, IL   1980–1981
Instructor

MERCY HOSPITAL AND MEDICAL CENTER, CHICAGO, IL   1979–1980
Staff Nurse, ICU

RUSH-PRESBYTERIAN-ST. LUKE'S MEDICAL CENTER, CHICAGO, IL   1978–1979
Staff Nurse, SICU

EDUCATION/LICENSURE

MSN, 1982, Rush University College of Nursing, Chicago, IL
BSN, 1978, Saint Xavier University School of Nursing, Chicago, IL
Registered Nurse, State of Illinois

COMPUTER SKILLS

WordPerfect, Word, Excel, PowerPoint, Access

Cover Letters

Each time you mail your resume, it must be accompanied by a one-page personalized cover letter. This cover letter directs the reader to your credentials, and gives you a chance to explain why you are interested in a particular position and organization. Your cover letter allows you to target the specific aspects of your background that correspond to the specific needs of an employer. The more you know about the organization or person to whom you are writing, the more you can focus on what will genuinely interest the reader. Your cover letter should be written to a specific person. If a name is not listed in an ad, call the organization and ask to whom your letter should be addressed.

In addition, your resume and cover letter are the first opportunity for an employer to learn about you. Thus, they must be perfectly typed in standard business form (see examples below) on high-quality paper and contain no spelling or grammatical errors. Purchase extra blank sheets of your resume paper so your resume and cover letters can be printed on matching paper.

Content

Your cover letter should cover these four general areas.

Introduction/Why You Are Writing. Always mention the position, the organization, how you learned about it, and your current status. For example, you might write: "I was interested to read in the *Washington Post* that the George Washington Hospital is looking for a surgical intensive care unit nurse. I will receive my BSN degree from Case Western University in May and I am eager to be considered for the position," or "Dr. Jane Jones told me that the Blue Ridge Family Practice will be hiring a pediatric nurse specialist, and I am writing to express my interest in the position. I will be graduating from the University of Pittsburgh School of Nursing in August with an MSN degree in child-care and pediatrics."

If you are sending resumes to organizations that have not formally advertised positions—you will wish to include information on why you are writing and refer to your current status. For example, "I am sending you a copy of my resume with the hope that the East Orange Family Practice will have a vacancy for a nurse practitioner. In August, I will complete my master's degree in nursing with a specialization in family health at Yale University."

What Your Experience/Education Offers. Highlight the special things in your background and on your resume that make you the right candidate for the position. You do not need to repeat everything that is already on your resume. Just pick the aspects of your background that will be most interesting to the individual employer, and be direct about emphasizing your particular accomplishments.

If, for example, an advertisement for a psychiatric nurse stresses supervisory ability, you might write: "As my enclosed resume indicates, I have had broad clinical experience as a psychiatric nurse. In addition, during the five years I was on the staff of St. Elizabeth's Psychiatric Hospital, I was promoted from staff nurse to primary nurse. As primary nurse, I trained and supervised twelve psychiatric aides, all whom have remained on staff and have been promoted to technician positions."

Why You are Interested in the Position and the Organization. It is appropriate to say something about why you want a particular job and want to work for the particular employer. For example, if you are interested in a nursing position in a large, university-affiliated hospital, you might say something like: "My clinical rotations at Georgetown Medical Center and the George Washington Hospital Center have impressed upon me the value of practicing nursing in a teaching hospital. I am especially interested in becoming involved in ongoing research, and feel that teaching hospitals provide the best opportunities for such work."

If you have enough specific information about the position and the organization to do so, it is a good idea to stress how and why your experience and interest meet the organization's needs—why this is a good fit. This paragraph (or section of the previous paragraph) lets the reader know that you've done your homework, and that you are familiar with their organization.

What Will Happen Next? This is your chance to structure what you hope the next steps will be. You can indicate interest in an interview, and prepare the reader for the fact that you may follow up your letter with a phone call to find out the status of your application. Maintain as much control as possible. Ending a cover letter with "I look forward to hearing from you," while perfectly appropriate, requires that the employer take the next step. You are better off taking the initiative by calling the employer to schedule an interview, if you feel comfortable doing so.

Other Cover Letter Pointers. All employers want, and all positions require, people with excellent communications skills. Your cover letter demonstrates your writing skills, so compose it thoughtfully. Allow your personality to come through, and be sure to express interest and enthusiasm, about both what you have to offer and what they offer you. Although this is a formal letter, the style doesn't need to be stiff. You should try to be creative in your cover letter to stimulate an employer's interest without jeopardizing the professional presentation of your qualifications.

A good cover letter will communicate your interest, motivation, and self-confidence and increase the likelihood of both a close reading of your resume and an interview.

Sample Cover Letters

Sample Cover Letter 1: Applicant with BSN/MSN Degree
Seeking Position in Systems/Technical Positions

Alter Ames
Address
Phone number
Email address

February 25, 2002

James Quan
Director of Human Resources
Calzon Medical Systems
Address

Dear Mr. Quan:

I am interested in a position with Calzon Medical Systems Corporation. I became interested in the company through my current work at the University of California at San Francisco Health System where I am part of the implementation team installing Calzon's clinical computing system, PRQ9000. After implementing the Calzon system for our health center, I am certain that I would like to contribute to your efforts at the home base. My work history of four years of clinical nursing experience sets me apart from other information system specialists working in the health care field and is complemented by my undergraduate education in Information Systems.

As an Applications Specialist for the PRQ clinical computing system, I provide direct support to hospital system users in its implementation throughout the center. I troubleshoot computer system and PRQ-specific problems, providing a link between information systems professionals and hospital units. I also provide training, assess technology effectiveness and develop protocols and guidelines for users. With several years of service as a staff nurse, I am particularly adept at instructing users with clinical backgrounds.

My dual interests in health care information systems and nursing were nurtured with a Bachelor of Science in Information Systems from UC Berkeley that I earned in 1991 and a Bachelor of Science in Nursing that I earned from UCSF in 1995. To enhance my skills and expertise in technology and nursing, I returned to school in 1996 to pursue a Master of Nursing Administration.

I am very enthusiastic about opportunities with Calzon. I hope that we can talk about possible positions when I am in Los Angeles during the week of April 5. I will call next week to discuss convenient times for our meeting.

Very Truly Yours,

Alter Ames

Sample Cover Letter 2: Letter of Application and Introduction, Recent BSN Graduate Expresses a Preference of Departments

Bryn Mathers
Address
Phone number
Email address

August 2, 2002

Ms. Donna Bailin
Nurse Recruiter
Memorial Health System
Address

Dear Ms. Bailin:

I am writing to express my interest in exploring employment opportunities with Memorial Health System. As a recent BSN graduate of the Purdue University Calumet, Department of Nursing, I have had the opportunity to work in several clinical settings, including my current clinical practicum on the AIDS and oncology unit at Memorial Health System. While I would ideally like to work with oncology patients, I would like to be considered for any staff nursing positions that may be available. I am willing to work all shifts, including evenings and weekends.

Last summer, I worked as a Nurse Extern on a medical/surgical floor at St. Margaret Mercy Healthcare Center in Hammond. This experience allowed me to implement and strengthen my nursing skills and provided a broad base of exposure to a variety of patients. This semester I am conducting my twenty-hour-a-week senior leadership project at Memorial Health System. I am working on the dedicated AIDS and oncology unit and gaining exposure to other outstanding aspects of Memorial. Through these experiences, I am observing first-hand the excellent quality of and the cooperative multidisciplinary approach to patient care as well as the progressive techniques that are trademarks of Memorial Health System.

In addition to my nursing skills, I have demonstrated leadership at school. My extracurricular activities include mentoring underclass nurses, and leading the Student Nurse's Association as its most recent President. Balancing course work, clinical experiences, and extracurricular involvement required commitment, time management, and, at times, my well-regarded sense of humor.

I would be delighted to begin my nursing career with Memorial Health System. I will contact you the week of September 10th to see if we can arrange a time to meet for an interview. I look forward to meeting you.

Sincerely,

Bryn Mathers

Sample Cover Letter 3: Second Degree Graduate/Approach Referring to a Mutual Friend, Moving from Staff Nurse Position to Nurse Practitioner Position

Joan Jacobs
Address

March 15, 2000

Susan Teilens, Nurse Manager
Physicians' Practices of Jewish Memorial Hospital
Address

Dear Ms. Teilens:

My current supervisor at Beth Israel Deaconess Medical Center, Martha Crayne, suggested that I contact you about a possible job opportunity with the Physician's Practices of Jewish Memorial Hospital. Martha and I have worked together since I graduated from the Gerontological Nurse Specialist Program at Boston College School of Nursing in 1997. Coming to nursing education following a liberal arts degree from Smith College in 1994, I completed the BSN/MSN Program with the specialty in Gerontology in three years.

Although my title at Beth Israel is staff nurse, my responsibilities have included many aspects of the nurse practitioner's role. As Martha can confirm, I chose to serve as a staff nurse to add depth to my experience before seeking employment as an autonomous nurse practitioner. In my work at Beth Israel, I have enhanced my strong clinical skills including assessment, diagnostics, and collaborative abilities. In my current setting, I have taken on many of the responsibilities of the nurse practitioner's role.

I am excited about the possibility of taking the next step and assuming the title and complete responsibilities of a nurse practitioner with the Physicians' Practices of Jewish Memorial Hospital. My maturity, education, clinical training and experience have prepared me for the role.

I hope that we can talk about the position of nurse practitioner that will soon become available in your practice. Perhaps we can meet during the first week of April while I am attending a conference nearby at the Pie Cultural Center. I will contact you next week to see about your availability. My resume is enclosed.

Warm regards from Martha.

Yours truly,

Joan Jacobs

Enclosure

Sample Cover Letter 4: Follow-Up Letter After Meeting Recruiter at Job Fair

Heather Marshall
Address

May 19, 1999

Roberta T. Smith, Nursing Recruiter
Children's Memorial Hospital
Address

Dear Ms. Smith:

On Friday, May 15th, I had a conversation with you at the health care job fair in the Chicago Convention Center. My interest in serving children at Children's Memorial Hospital as a registered nurse in the outpatient clinic was strengthened by your description of the position.

My experience with children in outpatient settings is extensive. For the last three years, I have worked in the Martha S. Calbert Outpatient Center of the Northwestern University Healthcare Network, where I assessed children and families at time of intake and effectively saw them through procedures from introduction and understanding of procedures to training for at-home care. I also act as the liaison between the clinic and discharged patient families.

Before coming to the Calbert Center, my nursing experience included home-care visits to families of children with diabetes. In this role at Rush-Presbyterian-St. Luke's Medical Center, I also provided information and training to caretakers. Over the last few years, I have found great satisfaction in my work with children and families in outpatient settings and would like very much to continue this avenue of work with Children's Memorial Hospital.

I enjoyed talking with you last week and I look forward to further discussions. During the first week of June, I will call to establish a convenient time for us to meet.

Thank you for your consideration. I have enclosed another resume for your reference.

Sincerely,

Heather Marshall

Sample Cover Letter 5: Letter of Introduction from BSN Moving to Another City, Changing Fields; Has Acquaintance in Common with Recruiter

Margaret Maloney
Address
Phone number Email address
May 21, 2003

Kadisha Smiley
Nurse Recruiter
Naples Hospital
Address

Dear Ms. Smiley:

I am writing at the suggestion of Dr. Max Truman Smith, with whom I became acquainted while we were both working in New York City. During the time that Max and I collaborated on a project involving a major New York medical system, he learned that I was moving to Florida and he told me about the high quality and personalized nursing care at the Naples Hospital. I have recently moved to Collier County and I am seeking a position as a registered nurse. Although I am especially interested in the emergency department, I will gladly consider any available positions for a registered nurse.

In 1996, I earned a Bachelor of Science in Nursing degree from Columbia University and have recently applied for a Florida nursing license. My clinical experiences as a nursing student included two rotations in major medical center emergency rooms and other units as well as other nursing roles in community hospital settings. At the Columbia Presbyterian Medical Center and the New York University Medical Center I had the opportunity to participate in numerous clinical procedures and was exposed to a wide range of medical disorders. While serving in the St. Francis Health Consortium Hospital, I gained a flavor for the special service and personalized care of community hospitals. It is this combination of experiences and interests that sparks my desire to join in your efforts at Naples Hospital.

My education at Columbia University included dual majors in Nursing and Economics with an emphasis on Health Care Management. Following graduation, I worked in New York as an Analyst in the area of health care finance where I evaluated the financial structures of health care businesses. Although I enjoy the overview of health care institutions from the business and financial perspective, I long to serve patients in a more direct way as an RN. During the two years I worked in New York in finance, I maintained my nursing licensure, took a course at NYU in emergency medicine and volunteered in a community health clinic where I assessed patients and prepared recommendations for their treatment. At the community health clinic, many of the patients were elderly.

I will call you the week of June 14th to see if we can establish a time to meet. I am anxious to talk with you and to resume my nursing career in direct patient care. My resume is attached.

Thank you for your kind consideration.

Sincerely,

Margaret Maloney

Sample Cover Letter 6: Nurse Practitioner Relocating/Colleague Referral

May 8, 2001

Caryn Carrier, Nurse Recruiting
Memorial Sloan-Kettering Cancer Center
Address

Dear Ms. Carrier:

I am writing to express my interest in the Pediatric Oncology Clinical Specialist position that may be available at Memorial Sloan-Kettering Cancer Center. My colleague, Alleis Locovara, a former Sloane Kettering nurse, recommended that I contact you about this possibility. I will complete the Pediatric Oncology Advanced Practice Nurse Program at the University of Minnesota in August 2001 and I am extremely interested in exploring the opportunity to work with you.

Currently an employee in the Children's Division of Hematology and Oncology at the University of Minnesota Medical Center, I also recently completed a twelve-week clinical rotation in Pediatric Oncology at the Mayo Clinic. Employment in oncology and school clinicals in the field have broadened and enhanced my base of knowledge of oncologic disease processes and their specific treatments. I am confident of my clinical skills and decision-making abilities.

I have also learned that effective treatment of cancer patients takes a special sensitivity and a set of skills outside the clinical realm. I believe that Memorial Sloan-Kettering Cancer Center serves patients and their families with sensitivity and conveys an attitude of appreciation for what each day of life has to offer. I adhere to the philosophy that nursing professionals make a difference in patient's lives with compassionate, positive and energetic attitudes toward patient care.

My goal is to serve on the Memorial Sloan-Kettering Cancer Center nursing team and to join the leaders in the field. I believe that I have a great deal to contribute and I appreciate your consideration. My resume is enclosed.

Sincerely,

Erica Arturi
Address
Phone number
Email address

Sample Cover Letter 7: Nursing Administration

JESSICA D. ERIN
Address
Phone number Email address

March 1, 2002

Marissa Able
Director, Human Resources
Vanderbilt Center for Gerontology
Address

Dear Ms. Able:

I am interested in the position as Director of Health Services that was advertised in the *Nashville Blade* last Sunday. A recent Master's graduate from the Health Care Administration Program at Emory University, I have also served for five years in clinical nursing and nursing management roles. I hope to contribute my clinical and administrative skills to the Vanderbilt Center for Gerontology.

As part of my Master's work, I shadowed a nursing home administrator for six weeks, developing a clear understanding of the responsibilities and routines of the role. For the Atlanta Gerontology Center, I created a project in which I evaluated patient health services and delivery systems and prepared recommendations for changes. The advice I offered was accepted and implemented to the satisfaction of staff and administrators currently using my suggestions.

In my nursing roles at Atlanta Memorial Hospital over the last five years, I assumed many management responsibilities. I trained and supervised two student nurses from Emory University and evaluated the performance of a new staff nurse in the unit. I was selected to serve on the Credentials and Certification committee of the hospital from which decisions were made to alter scheduling procedures. Although I was called a Staff Nurse, I performed duties associated with a nurse manager.

I will be moving to Nashville in June 2002 and expect to look for housing in the area between April 15 and April 25. I will call you next week to see if there is a convenient time for us to meet while I am in Nashville next month. My resume is enclosed for your perusal.

Thank you for your consideration.

Sincerely,

Jessica D. Erin

Sample Cover Letter 8: Nursing Administration Graduate Seeking Consulting Position

June 15, 2002

Christopher Eugene, Manager
Health Care Division
David and Benson Consulting
Address

Dear Mr. Eugene:

In the June Issue of the *Hartford Union News* I learned that you are seeking a Consultant in your Health Care Division. This opportunity interests me very much since I have worked in health care services and administration for seven years and have recently completed a number of business courses in order to refine my analytical, computing, and quantitative skills.

With a combination of health care experience and recent business coursework, I am a unique candidate. A graduate of the University of Pennsylvania, I completed a Bachelor of Science degree in Nursing. While practicing as a Staff Nurse, I assumed leadership through administrative roles that kept me attuned to policy and management decision-making. I volunteered for a position as a committee person for Employee Health and Safety, Staff Education, Ethical Practices and Cost-containment committees at the hospital. I was selected as unit representative to the Quality Assessment team and voluntarily wrote the report of survey data that administrators rely on to assess effectiveness of service delivery. My coursework in business included courses in accounting, systems, medical administration and comparative health systems strategies. This combination of direct health care expertise and business strategies strengthened my knowledge of the health care marketplace and its internal dynamics.

In addition to my health care experience, my communications, analytical and quantitative abilities will allow me to be a strong, dynamic and knowledgeable member of your health care consulting team. My resume is enclosed for your consideration. I will contact you next week to plan a time for us to meet.

Thank you,

Genevieve Eleanor Morgan
Address
Phone number
Email address

Sample Cover Letter 9: Recent BSN Graduate Applying for a Non-Nursing Management Training Program

June 3, 2002

Andrea Wallace, Manager
Management Training Programs
Procter and Gamble
Address

Dear Ms. Wallace:

As a recent graduate of the University of Kentucky, I was attracted to the web-site description of the Procter and Gamble Management Training Program. I am interested in rotating through the many departments of Procter and Gamble and in participating in departmental operations. Please send me application materials for the training class that begins in September 2002.

My educational background is rich and diverse. I earned a Bachelor of Science in Nursing degree with high honors from the University of Kentucky in May 2002. In addition to excellent clinical nursing experience and scientific coursework, my nursing education included a strong course of study in the liberal arts. My study of sciences and direct application of nursing practices was complemented by experience in research, followed by the writing of effective papers and oral presentation of outcomes to classmates. A broad-based education with emphasis on science and communications, both directly with people, as well as in writing, lends strength to my ability to be flexible and creative in my thinking.

In addition to clinical rotations in large health care organizations, work experience has enriched my ability to view an organization's departmental and overall effectiveness. During my four years of college, I worked twenty hours each week in a work-study position. By performing administrative tasks in the Career Services Office, I learned the importance of organizational work. I maintained databases, generated outcomes from survey data and helped organize career fairs. The regular job, along with coursework, also contributed to my ability to manage my time effectively. For several summers, I served in a medical center where I rotated from admissions, to transportation, to phlebotomy, to surgery, gaining an overview of departmental roles and an opportunity to see how each department contributes to the effectiveness of the whole.

I am very enthusiastic about joining the training program at Procter and Gamble. Experience in each of the major departments will allow me to gain an overview of the operation and to understand how each component contributes to the organization in its own unique way.

Thank you for your consideration. I look forward to seeing the application materials.

Yours truly,

Kelley O'Malley
Address
Phone number   Email address

Follow-Up Correspondence

After every interview (whether for an actual position or for information only) send a thank-you letter. Even if you did not enjoy the interview (or the interviewer), and/or you are not interested in the position, it is important to thank the interviewer for the time she or he spent with you. You never know whether, five years from now, that person will be in a position to hire you for a job you would really like.

In addition to writing thank you letters, it is also standard practice to send a letter when you accept a position and when you have decided that you no longer wish to be considered (see samples on following pages). None of the letters need to be long and elaborate—the vital thing is to compose a well-written letter and to send it immediately after your interview.

Content. Address the letter to the person who initially invited you for the interview. If you saw more than one person, you can write to each of them, or refer to them in your letter to the primary interviewer. Mention the title of the position for which you interviewed.

If you are interested in the position, express your enthusiasm and reiterate your desire for the job and your qualifications for it. You may want to add information or materials (such as reference letters) that enhance your candidacy. You may also refer to the discussion that occurred in the interview. If a timeframe for their decision was discussed, you may also mention the date that you hope to hear from them. Basically, you want to express thanks for the time the employer spent with you.

If you are not interested, you can still express appreciation for being considered and for the courtesy extended to you. If you can imagine no circumstances under which you would accept the position, you should not continue with the process. Thus, if you've decided to withdraw yourself from the applicant pool, this would be a good time to put that in writing. Try to give a reason for your withdrawal that will leave you on good terms with the interviewer (see examples below).

Sample Thank-You Note 1

DC Allen
Address
May 21, 2002

Orell Jackson
Senior Analyst
Bear Stearns
Address

Dear Mr. Jackson:

I value the time we spent together yesterday discussing your role as a Health Care Analyst. I am excited about the possibility of learning more about the field and possibly applying to positions at Bear Stearns in New York after graduation.

My studies in Health Care Management at the Anderson School of Business coupled with my degree in Nursing from UCLA, give me tools similar to those that you have used in your analyst position. As you suggested, I will talk with Professor Reshefski about including additional coursework in finance in my current curriculum.

Thank you again for taking the time to share your ideas and offer suggestions as to how I may wish to proceed in reaching my goals. I will follow-up with your colleague Christopher Neighbors.

Your trip to the Hamptons sounds lovely. Have a great time.

Sincerely,

DC Allen

Sample Thank-You Note 2

Mai On
Address

March 15, 2002

Margarita Owen, Nurse Recruiter
Chicago Children's Medical Center
Address

Dear Ms. Owen:

Thank you for meeting with me last Tuesday to talk about possible positions at the Chicago Children's Medical Center. After serving in major pediatric medical centers in the northeast for the last five years, I offer expertise, maturity and devoted service to children. As I mentioned, I am very enthusiastic about my move to Chicago in the spring. My sister attended North Park University, which gave me the chance to visit Chicago frequently and to know and love the city. Chicago Children's Medical Center is my first choice of employers.

I enjoyed perusing your web site, as you suggested that I would, and I spoke to the Nurse Managers in the NICU and PICU, as well. The emphasis on team building and collegiality among staff members is impressive. Chicago Children's serves children and families from a wide range of socioeconomic groups and fits the values of patient-centered care through teamwork that are important to me. I hope that you will consider me as openings become available. Another resume is enclosed for your convenience.

I will be in touch with you in May to let you know of my continued interest and to see if you have learned of openings.

With sincere thanks,

Mai On

Sample Thank-You Note 3

April 5, 2002

Ms. Sun-Yee Choi
Nurse Recruiter
Potomac Hospital
Address

Dear Ms. Choi,

Thank you for meeting with me last Tuesday to discuss my interest in nursing positions at Potomac Hospital. It was kind of you to spend time talking with me, even though you have no openings at this time.

Completion of my nursing education at George Mason University has prepared me to take the NCLEX exam, which I will complete in June; I am anxious to serve as a staff nurse, once I am officially an RN.

As a new resident of nearby Dumfries, I am especially interested in serving in a nursing role in the area and in a community-based hospital. I appreciate your willingness to keep me in mind if openings arise.

Yours truly,

Ortis Washington
Address

Sample Thank-You Note 4

August 2, 2002

Jesse Nover, Nurse Recruiter
Office of Human Resources
Metro Health System
Address

Dear Mr. Nover:

I appreciate the time you took to talk with me recently about possible openings in your nursing department. It was kind of you to make yourself available at the last minute.

My year of experience as a Staff Nurse at St. Andrews Hospital has prepared me to work with patients with pulmonary concerns, especially chronic asthma. My school clinicals also included experience teaching at-home care to parents of children with asthma. My interests are broad, however, and if openings are not available in pulmonary care, I am interested in working in any unit in which you need me.

After we talked, I spent some time visiting wards and activity rooms in the medical center. I was impressed with the warm feeling that I got from every aspect of hospital services, from the cafeteria to the arts and crafts room. I hope that you will consider me for a staff nurse position.

Sincerely yours,

Brion Jiang
Address

Sample Letters Accepting and Declining Offers

Use your own letterhead, which includes your name, address, and contact information. Use the contact person's name, title, and complete address. See letters above for complete models.

Sample Acceptance 1

With pleasure, I accept your offer of a position as Nurse Practitioner at the Berkely Healthcare Center. I am anxious to receive written confirmation of your verbal offer and the verification of benefits that we discussed.

I look forward to the orientation session that will begin on May 15th at 9 a.m. in the Forster Auditorium. Ms. Robinson of Human Resources let me know about the opportunity to attend this introductory session.

Thank you for the time you took to work with me on the details of my employment and for giving me a feel for the Center.

Sample Acceptance 2

I am very enthusiastic about joining your staff in May and write to confirm my acceptance of the position as Nurse Educator. It was a pleasure to receive your call yesterday offering me the position.

I believe that our shared interests in serving the community as health educators through the Community Health Alliance will allow us to reach a wide range of clients previously underserved. I look forward to being a member of your team.

Sample Acceptance 3

Thank you for your call to confirm the job offer as Emergency Room Nurse. I look forward to the chance to serve in El Paso. Thanks too for your willingness to be flexible on my start date. As you know, I have a long-standing plan to travel during the month of August and will begin the new position on September 1, 2003.

Our shared interests in working with Spanish-speaking clients and in expanding emergency services are of pressing importance. I am excited about working with you and I am enthusiastic about advocating for additional funding for the program.

Sample Decline 1

Thank you so much for taking the time to meet with me last week about the position as Nurse Practitioner with the Waldorf Family Practice. It was very nice to meet you and your colleagues to discuss your need for a geriatric specialist.

As you know, my experience and interests lie in working with a wider range of ages and I hope to work in a setting where my primary population includes young people. I am sorry that our needs do not mesh at this time. I appreciate your interest in me and I gave the offer strong consideration, primarily because your staff impressed me with their thoughtful questions and supportive demeanors. Surely our paths will cross again since we live in neighboring communities.

Best of luck in your search for a practitioner with special interest in working with the elderly. I appreciate your interest in me.

Sample Decline 2

Thank you so much for the time and energy that you spent on my behalf. I am glad that I had the chance to meet you and your colleagues at Lancaster Family Practice and I hope that we will meet again. This letter is to extend my appreciation to you and to your staff and to let you know that I must decline your offer of employment.

As you know, I have interviewed with several practice groups and have accepted the position with the Bird-In-Hand Family Practice where I will contribute to the special care of Amish children with congenital maladies. Even though, I liked your group very much and found it difficult to make the decision, my long-standing interest in issues of public health was the deciding factor for me.

Warm regards and many thanks for your consideration.

Sample Decline 3

This note is to let you know that I am unable to accept your offer of a position as Staff Nurse. I have accepted another position in a neighboring hospital where I will be serving as a Nurse Manager.

Thank you for taking the time to talk with me about openings at Wake Forest University Baptist Medical Center. It was thoughtful of you to provide a tour of the hospital and to introduce me to nurse managers on several floors. I look forward to seeing you again in the future.

I also appreciate your efforts to help me become oriented to the Winston-Salem area. Through your vivid and helpful suggestions for good restaurants, my husband and I happily celebrated our anniversary at the Winslow House last week.

Sample Decline 4

At your web site, I recently completed the online application for position # 322. I am writing to let you know that I have accepted a position in another health care organization and would like to withdraw my application from consideration for the Staff Nurse position at Rhoades Hospital.

Perhaps we will be able to work together at some time in the future. Best of luck to you in your search for a Staff Nurse.

Sample Decline 5

Thank you for considering me for a nursing position with your practice. Although I appreciate your interest in my application, I am uneasy about the length of the commute to your office from my Spokane home. With this in mind, I must decline your offer of employment.

It was good to meet you, and I thank you for your consideration.

Sample Decline 6

Thank you for your interest in my application as Staff Nurse at Oregon State Medical Center. I write to ask that you withdraw my name from consideration for the position at this time. I have made the decision to stay in New York City to complete the project that I began on teen suicide in conjunction with other nurses here. Although I am not able to make the transition this spring, my desire to come to Oregon to live near my family is powerful. By next fall, when the project is complete, I will feel free to relocate. At that time, I will contact you and hope that you will consider me for another position.

Sample Decline 7

Thank you for taking the time to interview me last week for a position as Staff Nurse. I appreciate the time you took to talk with me and to answer my questions about the position.

After our meeting, I made a decision to continue to serve in my current position for another year to gain more experience before I move to a new facility. Although the job you described is very attractive and I feel that I got a good sense of your staff, I believe that taking another year in my present job as Nurse Educator best facilitates my professional growth.

Thank you again for meeting with me.

Sample Decline 8

Thank you for meeting with me over the last few weeks to discuss the Nurse Manager position at St. Johns. You have given generously of your time and energy and I appreciate your efforts on my behalf. I enjoyed getting to know you and I know that I would like working with you.

Even though I would prefer to work in a smaller facility with a Catholic orientation, I have accepted a job with pay scales and benefits that are more in keeping with my economic needs. As a family breadwinner, I must consider salary and benefits in my decision-making.

I appreciate your recommendation that I continue our talks by meeting the CEO to confirm my job offer, but, with reluctance, I must decline.

Thank you again for your thoughtfulness. I am glad that we will be working in the same community and I hope to see you at association or professional development meetings.

4
Interviewing Techniques

Effective job search strategies, along with well-written resumes and cover letters, may lead to the most important step toward obtaining a job: an interview. The ideal interview is a two-way street, allowing the employer to convey information to you, the interviewee, about the job and the organization, while you have the opportunity to discuss your qualifications and amplify items from your resume. The interview is the most important element in the job search process. It is a time to assess the "match" between you and the employer. The employer will be assessing your background, skills, personal style, and interest in the position and organization and will also be supplying you with information. You will be telling the interviewer about your skills, your level of commitment, and your experiences, while finding out whether or not the particular job/organization is right for you.

An invitation to interview generally means that the potential employer believes that you are qualified to do the job. Stand back and congratulate yourself on a job well done. This also means that your cover letter and resume or networking skills were effective. An interviewer will not take time to meet with a person whose qualifications are of no interest or are obviously lacking. The interview, therefore, will not determine your qualifications for the job, but will be a chance for the interviewer to find out what you're like and to assess how well you would fit into the organization. It is quite common and natural to be nervous before an interview. Typically, once you get into the interview room and settle down, you will realize that you are just having a conversation with a colleague in the field. You've gotten to this stage on your own merits. Keep up the good work!

The basic rule of thumb of interviews is that you need to articulate convincingly why you should be hired and why you are interested in the position. The following qualities will enhance your ability to come across professionally and effectively in an interview.

Communication skills. The ability to write and articulate ideas and information and to interact effectively with others.

Confidence. An awareness of your strengths and weaknesses (areas in which you hope to grow/add skills). Willingness to set and attain realistic goals.

Personality. A sense of humor, cheerfulness, and flexibility in new situations. Enthusiasm to accept challenges is particularly important.

Accomplishments. Academic and professional, as well as personal achievements.

Knowledge. An understanding of the organization and the career field.

General Pointers

Be prepared. Know as much about the position/hospital/organization as you can. The more you know, the more focused your answers will be. Ask for a copy of the annual report, informational brochure, or job description prior to the interview. Ask colleagues, friends, and faculty about the organization. Libraries have many guides to hospitals, health care consulting firms, private agencies, professional associations, and other categories, in which you can get general information on organizations of interest. Web sites provide tremendous amounts of information. You may, for example, go directly to hospital web sites in the United States and around the world at neuro-www.mgh.harvard.edu/hospitalweb.shtml or to www.pharmweb.net for links to pharmaceutical company home pages. (See sections in Chapter 2 entitled "Identify Opportunities" and "Research Your Target Area.") Don't forget to seek personal contacts through networking resources!

In your conversation with possible employers, be sure to emphasize your potential for high-level professional accomplishments. Mention your skills in teambuilding, delegating, and leadership. Think of examples from clinical experiences, school leadership, community service, or other jobs that demonstrate your leadership potential. Employers often hire for potential—especially in new nurses; aides can accomplish basic tasks like taking vital signs. A nurse who can manage complicated situations with ease is a great asset to the team.

Know yourself. Think honestly about your strengths and weaknesses (areas for growth), your work style, skills, and goals. Be prepared to give honest answers. Review your resume critically and try to identify the areas that an employer might view as limitations without apologizing for deficiencies. Think about how you can answer difficult questions accurately and positively to enhance your qualifications for a job.

For example, if you are returning to the work force after raising a family for ten years, an employer might ask questions to determine the effect that this lack of recent employment might have on your ability to perform the job. If you have worked on a per-diem basis for a home health agency during this ten-year period, that level of professional involvement might strengthen your application; be certain to mention it.

Perhaps you are seeking an administrative position and you have not held a management job. You will think through tasks you have performed that involved management, assessment, and organizational skills that were performed under other job titles. You would also emphasize your recent nursing administration coursework and field projects and your positive feedback from the organization with which you worked. Thinking through these issues in advance will also enable you to come up with effective answers to describe your past in a professional way. This is impressive.

Be prompt and professional. Arrive early. If you don't know where the organization is located, call for directions ahead of time. Anticipate traffic, parking problems, and general unforeseen difficulties. If you find that you are going to be late, be sure to call and let someone know. To be more comfortable, you should arrive approximately ten minutes early. Allow yourself the time to read your resume one more time, catch your breath, hang up your coat, and get into an enthusiastic frame of mind for the interview.

Dress appropriately. Wear clothes befitting a person employed in the organization where you hope to work; you should be comfortable and feel you look your best. In general, you need not be confined to the standard gray flannel business suit; however, you should look conservative and professional. For women: a skirt and jacket, dress, or often a nice pants suit are fine. For men: a suit and tie, or jacket and slacks, are recommended. You can err by dressing too formally, dressing too casually, or being too trendy. Keep adornments and fragrances to a minimum. As part of a dress code, some hospitals have policies prohibiting visible body piercing except in the ear, for example. Be aware of having clean, clear, or lightly colored fingernails and fresh-looking attire, including footwear. Although some health care workplaces are flexible with personal style differences, color and style uniformity in daily apparel determined by unit or floor is still the norm. An interview is not the time to express your individuality. Wear conservative attire in an interview and emphasize a personal fit. A first impression is possible only once. Make that impression a positive, professional one.

Be honest. Let an employer get to know you. An interview is a time to exchange information and ideas and to get a feeling for whether the match is right for both of you. You want to be sure that you and the employer know what to expect if you are hired. It is not advisable, however, to reveal personal problems, family complications, or uncertainties or to point out problem issues in past employment.

Be positive. Never say anything negative about past experiences, employers, courses, or professors. Employers, like anyone, tend to generalize: if you didn't like "x," you are a negative person and won't like me either. Figure out what was positive about an experience and talk about that. Be "up" about yourself. If you wouldn't hire yourself, neither will the interviewer. Be enthusiastic. If you are genuinely interested in the job, let the interviewer know that. There is no need to sound desperate, just interested. This interest makes the interviewer feel as though his or her organization is well respected and enticing, which is flattering.

Demonstrate interest. Research the organization prior to the interview, and ask questions during the interview about the job, the organization, and the people it serves. When asking questions, be sure that the answers will give you information that you don't already have (or should have) and that the questions are genuinely of interest to you. Be responsive to what has gone on in the interview. If you have listened well, you should be able to come up with thoughtful questions that impress the interviewer. See the list of sample questions. You may want to prepare a few questions in advance, but an insightful comment based on your conversation can make an even stronger statement.

Be ready for anything! Interviews in health care settings, in addition to the traditional one-on-one format, may involve speaking with several interviewers at once, meeting with different staff members successively, or even observing the setting for some length of time. If you meet with several interviewers at the same time, ask each person what role they play in the practice or organization. Each one may have a different area of interest and therefore a different perspective. Look directly at each person during the conversation and address some answers to everyone in the room. Say goodbye to each individual as you leave. When meeting successively with interviewers, do not hesitate to repeat what you said to the previous person since the second interviewer will not have been privy to your first conversation. Also remember that each person approaches the meeting with the perspective of his or her own discipline or role in the group. The questions asked and the responses you present should be in relation to the perspective each individual brings to the meeting. You may, for example, have a different conversation with a nursing peer, with whom you would work side-by-side every day, than one you would have with the non-nurse office manager, or the clinical director.

In addition to unusual interview styles, you may find yourself in unusual places, like the nursing area of a ward, a laboratory, or a lunchroom. Interviewers may ask practical questions about how you would deal with particular patient needs, define medical terms, or manage unpleasant coworkers. Remain flexible, retain your sense of humor, and go with the flow of the interview. An interview may become another adventure.

Practice. Good interviewees aren't born; they're made. Make an appointment with your career counselor to role-play or try it with friends. Practice answering the sample interview questions. Rehearsing can make an enormous difference in your confidence and your ease at fielding questions.

Follow-up. Always write a thank-you note promptly following an interview. Mail your note within forty-eight hours. A handwritten or typed note on good notepaper or professional stationery is fine. A well-conceived email is also acceptable; be sure to draft it carefully and give it the same attention to detail that you would give a letter. See the section on follow-up correspondence (Chapter 3) for details and models.

Become Familiar with *Salary Ranges*

For staff nurse positions, the nurse recruiter will usually inform you of the salary for the position. These salaries are typically based on a combination of education and experience and are not flexible. When salary is not mentioned, the interviewee should not address the issue of compensation at the first meeting. Sometimes, an employer will ask YOU about your salary requirements, and preparation is the only way to meet this challenge effectively. It is wise to have researched salaries and determined a range of expectation before interviewing for a position. Anticipate the salary question, so that you are not caught unprepared. In addition, if the interviewer offers salary information about the position, you will be prepared to comment on your comfort with the range of salary that is proposed. If the proposed salary is within an appropriate range, you will know it. If the range that the employer mentions is lower than is acceptable to you, you may decide to address it at this time. Specific salary agreements are best left until the job is offered. By this time the employer has determined that you are the person for the job, wants you to join the staff and is committed to hiring you.

Salary information is available. Many universities and schools of nursing maintain salary surveys of graduating classes that can provide guidelines for you. Web sites and nursing journals provide salary information as well. Some sites that include salary information for health care careers are: http://www.nurse.net/salary/summary.shtml, www.bls.gov/oco/, www.salary.com, www.careerjournal.com, http://vir tualnurse.com, http://kcsun3.tripod.com/id116.htm, http://jobsmart. org/tools/salary/index.htm, www.wageweb.com, and www.ADVANCE forNP.com/npsalsurvey.html. For government pay rates check www. opm.gov/oca/payrates/index.htm. In addition to basic salaries, some employers offer additional compensation of varying types to encourage you to accept an offer. Also refer to "Negotiating" in Chapter 5.

Nursing salaries are sometimes expressed in hourly rates. To translate an hourly rate into an annual salary, multiply the hourly rate by 2,080. This shortcut is based on a forty-hour work week, multiplied by the fifty-two weeks of the year.

Telephone Interviews

When interested in positions outside your home area, you may be invited to interview in another region. Many employers will offer their resources to cover the cost of your visit. Others will not. It is appropriate to ask the potential employer if the organization is in a position to incur the costs for your travel. You could face a decision about whether to pay for travel to an interview with your personal funds.

Although traveling to the interview at your own expense demonstrates your strong interest in the job, it may not be financially feasible for you to fly cross-country for a screening interview. Let the employer know of your enthusiasm for the opportunity and that the travel expense would be a hardship for you. For screening purposes, a telephone interview may be a good way to have an initial conversation about your qualifications for the job and for you to get a feel for whether or not the position is a good match for your skills.

A first meeting is often a screening interview, whereby the employer (perhaps a nurse recruiter) meets with you to determine if you are a realistic candidate and a pleasant, appropriate person. The telephone interview is best for this kind of interaction. If, on the other hand, an employer is very enthusiastic about your credentials and your visit, has talked with those you chose to recommend you, and is arranging for you to meet a nurse manager (a decision-maker), your paying for the cross-country flight is probably the demonstration of interest that will help you get the job.

If a telephone screening is the appropriate choice for you, prepare for it in the same way that you would prepare for any other interview.

There are a few things that may be different, however. It will be important to arrange for a quiet, uninterrupted space in which to talk. Dress in work clothing, not nightclothes or jeans, and sit up in a comfortable position that will allow for interviewing posture. Your voice and demeanor will give a first impression. The way you are positioned and the way you are dressed will give you a more professional feeling that may be reflected in your voice. You will not have another chance for a first impression. Prepare your own questions and your answers to the commonly asked interview questions in the same way that you would for a face-to-face interview. Be sure that you sound enthusiastic, and speak slowly, loudly, and clearly. You may wish to practice on the phone with a friend. An advantage to a telephone interview is that you can refer to notes and to your resume during the conversation.

Occasionally, you will interview by phone with more than one person. In this case, ask the name and job title of each person participating in the conversation. Write down their names and titles; each participant will have a different perspective and it is important to know what disciplines they represent. Write a note to each person with whom you interview and meet the employer face-to-face when you can.

Sample Interview Questions and Answer Tips

Interview questions and styles vary as much as job titles. If you are interviewing for nonclinical positions, interview questions will vary accordingly. Following the sample questions for clinical interviews are some hints for nonclinical interviews.

Frequently Asked Questions for Clinical Positions

Tell me about yourself.
This is one of the most difficult questions to answer if you are unprepared; planning for it is a must. Keep your response short (a minute or less) and relevant. Give an overview of your nursing experience and/or education, highlighting in each instance special accomplishments, acquisition of new skills, or assumption of challenges. Take the opportunity to demonstrate your commitment to the field, describe your professional and extra-work contributions, and to exude your supportive collegial attitude. Be sure to speak positively about your experiences and about previous employers. Keep the response relevant to your career path and spiced with anecdotes of personal/extra curricular and professional contributions.

When did you know you wanted to be a nurse?
Perhaps you can describe the ways in which you explored your choice, or select an anecdote that shows why or how you made the decision to become a nurse. Trace a brief history of events that led to your decision. Include qualities that you value in nursing, like commitment, orientation to care for others, technical competencies, and a team-spirited approach to health care.

Why did you choose to study at _____?
Describe the strengths of your nursing program, your interests and contributions at school, or your local community commitments. Be sure to identify the positive outcomes of your choice.

Why did you choose to specialize in _____?
Choose a course, job, specific experience, or personal example that stimulated your interest in the specialty. Your discussion may include a series of factors. Mention factors that are exemplified by the best nurses in your discipline.

What are your strongest skills?
You may wish to choose a patient as an example and describe how you understood and dealt with the scientific or physiological factors as well as the social or emotional factors that affected the patient. You may wish to describe a creative approach to a patient's needs that required independent thinking and individualized care.

How would you describe yourself? How would a preceptor or colleague describe you?
Give examples of your behavior or descriptions of events that demonstrate that you are a strong team player. Describe extra duties that you have volunteered for or accepted; perhaps you can include examples of how you stretched yourself to meet organizational goals or to provide extraordinary service to patients. You may have special strength in showing compassion and understanding differences or in adjusting treatment plans to account for personal differences. Describe how you have done this.

Tell me about the most difficult clinical experience you've faced and how you handled it.
This question offers another opportunity to demonstrate by example how you assess a situation or patient, employ critical thinking, and apply previous experiences and education to solve a problem, or to collaborate with coworkers. This answer should be stated in a positive way, and what you learned from the challenging experience, as well as the outcome, should be included.

What do you consider the most important qualities a clinical nurse specialist/ nurse practitioner/nurse needs to do this job successfully?
In your description of important qualities include teamwork and collaboration, problem-solving abilities, orientation to good care and services, commitment and caring, in addition to a strong base of skills or experience. You may cite an example of an outstanding nursing professional you have observed.

What did you like best/least in your clinical experiences?
Discuss what you gained in a particular setting and why you value it now. This could include skills attained, methods explored, or supportive personal interactions. Remain positive and discuss what you gained from your least favorite experience too, even if a learning experience was challenging, turbulent, or not in your field of interest.

How did you motivate a resistant patient to comply with your instructions?
This is an opportunity to describe, in detail, how you evaluated a patient or situation, what strategies you developed to cope with the situation, and what the outcomes were. Engage the listener in a short story that has an ending.

What are your strengths and weaknesses?
Be specific about contributions you have made to your work or school environments. Identify your specific role by using examples. Addressing your weaknesses is challenging for many interviewees. Don't let this question stump you. Continue to be positive, just as when you describe a difficult work situation, by describing events as "challenges." Think through events in nursing school, in clinical experiences, or on the job where you have learned a hard lesson. What you learned from any ordeal and the outcome—how you currently handle similar situations—constitutes a significant and interesting answer.

Why are you interested in working for us?
Research the organization. See section in Chapter 2 entitled "Research and Contact Employers."

What gives you the most satisfaction as a nurse? Why?
Cite examples of experiences that provided satisfaction, extraordinary growth, insight, or challenge. Be sure to explain how this experience strengthened your resolve, enhanced your learning, added to your self-confidence, or enriched your life.

Where do you see yourself in five years?
You may wish to answer this in terms of skills or experiences you hope to acquire.

What two or three things are most important to you in your job?
If you are certain that you want a supportive team environment, an extremely organized workplace, close collaboration with nurse practitioners or other specific items, say so. Leaving your real preferences unstated can set you up for a disappointment in your new work environment. This question offers another opportunity to talk about what you value, like commitment, dedication to patient care, and sensitivity to individual needs.

What are some characteristics of the best nurse that you know?
Describe an outstanding nurse that you have observed. Discuss why you admire this person, bringing in important factors like teamwork and collaboration, unique contributions, extraordinary efforts to serve patients or the community, or demonstrations of commitment and caring.

What do you think is the most significant problem in health care today? What do you see as the major issues facing us in the future?
Read newspapers and professional journals to stay abreast of current issues and events in health care. What you choose as the most significant problem is less important than how you show your interest in the field and describe the issues that interest or confound you.

What do you enjoy doing when you're not working?
This is an opportunity to talk about what you do in your spare time. It allows a potential employer to get to know you a little better. It's probably a good idea not to mention if you take part in dangerous sports like motorcycling or hang-gliding. Be prepared for follow-up questions about your interests. If you mention sailing, for example, be prepared for follow-up questions about how you learned to sail, what type of boat you have, and where you go to sail it.

How do you relieve stress?
You may want to emphasize your personal health-related activities like exercise and pleasant relaxation techniques. It is certainly appropriate to discuss your interest in books, music, or other leisure activities, but be prepared to say specifically what books you read and what musicians you enjoy.

What would you do if . . . (cite a clinical situation)?
The interviewer is looking for your judgment and maturity in handling complex situations. You may have dealt with a similar circumstance, and you can describe what you did in that situation. You are expected to think carefully through the issues involved. The interviewer is not necessarily looking for one "right" answer; different nurses with good

judgment do not necessarily reach the same conclusion. Verbally share your thought process as you determine your answer; that way a potential employer gets a feel for your critical decision-making style.

Describe the best/worst supervisor you ever had.
Some supervisors mentor by offering good examples of excellent nursing care or discussing cases. Describe this type of supervisor if possible. Be certain not to criticize others but discuss what you learned from a different type of supervisor. Even an example of being left to fend for yourself offers learning opportunities for an enterprising nurse.

What are your salary requirements?
See the section "Become Familiar with Salary Ranges" above and be prepared for this question. See the section called "Negotiating" in Chapter 5 for suggestions about how to use the salary data.

Why should we hire you?
Be prepared for this question. Even if it's not asked directly, the answer to this should be woven throughout your responses. See tips above for a combination of factors that make you a terrific candidate for the position. You may wish to refer to the question about strengths and weaknesses.

Do you have any questions for me?
It's good to have a few questions to ask an interviewer:
Why is this position vacant? (don't sound argumentative—just curious)
What are the major responsibilities of this position? (if this hasn't been covered in interview)
Describe the ideal candidate for this position.
Who would be my supervisor and what is that person's supervisory style?
With whom would I collaborate on problem cases?
What do you see as the key issues/challenges facing the person in this job?
How would you describe a typical patient in this practice/facility?
What do you like most about your job and this organization?
How has this facility been affected by all the changes in the health care industry?
What is the time line for filling this position?
Will there be additional interviews?
When can I expect to hear from you?

Nonclinical Interviews

For nonclinical interviews, questions will vary widely. Know your industry and be prepared to discuss the topics you know will interest your interviewer. In pharmaceutical sales or consulting, for example, selling a product or service and educating others about what you offer is the objective. For these interviews, be prepared to market yourself, demonstrate your command of your health care subject matter, and show that you understand the value of marketing and sales. Even though most interviewers will want to see that you are articulate and knowledgeable about your own field and have the potential to sell a product or service, some consulting firms interview using the case method. Case questions are business-related questions, asking what you would do in a given health-related situation, around which you have a conversation with a recruiter to offer your thoughts, ideas, and opinions about the issues involved. The case method is designed to help the listener determine your level of skill in creative thinking and analysis. Good resources for learning about business interviewing and answering case-style questions are in the interview preparation section of the Boston Consulting Group at web site, www.bcg.com/careers/interview_prep/interview_prep.asp, and in print in *Vault.com Guide to the Case Interview* by Mark Asher and the staff of Vault.com (New York: Vault.com, 2000).

In behavioral interviewing, another type of interview that is popular with employers, specific questions are posed about how you would handle a given situation. The interviewer expects you to talk about how you have resolved similar problems or approached similar challenges in the past. This interviewing style is designed to determine, based on your previous behavior and experience, what kind of employee you will be and how you would handle yourself on the job.

5
The Job Offer

What Constitutes a Job Offer?

Following an interview, an employer may ask that you join the team or say that she or he would like to hire you. The verbal offer may come in person or by telephone. Congratulations on a successful interview! If you have an interest in the job, this is the time to express your enthusiasm for the position and the organization, as well as your appreciation for the invitation to join the team. Maintain the high level of excitement and enthusiasm during this conversation and set the stage for the next productive interaction. The conversation, including the verbal job offer from one enthusiastic interviewer, should not be considered a concrete offer of employment. It is appropriate to discuss "next steps" with the understanding that the job has not been officially offered. An actual job offer, which includes a salary figure and benefits package, should follow in a letter from the employer.

The first conversation about a job offer is not the time to negotiate, but to maintain the high level of interest. The salary subject could be broached, though, so see below for tips on how to handle it at this stage. A conversation about salary should come after an official offer is proffered and the facts on which to base your decision are in your hands. It is advisable not to accept a job on the spot, unless you have exhausted your research on salary and benefits and you are clear that this is, with certainty, the job that you want. In most cases, it is advisable to take time to think about the job and to go through the details of the work involved, the benefits package, and the advantages and disadvantages of the offer as a whole, before accepting.

In some cases, you may receive a verbal job offer and a salary offer at the same time. Because you have researched salaries and have a range of salary in mind (see Chapter 4), you may remark that the salary is a bit lower than you had expected, if this is true. If the salary offer is not quite what you hoped for, you may wish to say that the offer is in your range, but that you had hoped for more because of the average salaries for nursing graduates or for your special skills and experience. If you receive another offer from a competing employer and the salary offered is higher, you may say so. Say only what is true. Those with whom you are presently dealing may be your colleagues in the future. When possible, delay the salary conversation for a follow-up meeting (and be prepared with salary information).

An actual job offer includes salary and complete benefit information. Once you have received the offer (it should be in writing), it is appropriate to, once again, extend your thanks to the potential employer, express your enthusiasm for the job, and let the employer know that you will look over the entire package of information to be certain that the match is right for both of you. After you peruse the information about the job responsibilities and the employment package, develop a set of questions or points if you have issues to discuss. Do not ask a lot of piecemeal questions; gather all of your questions and issues of uncertainty and discuss them all at once in a prioritized way. See more about this in the section called "Negotiating" below.

Salary history. Employers will sometimes ask you about your salary history. If, for example, you are a recent graduate of a master's program and have worked part-time or in an RN position, or if you are changing fields, your salary history is not very relevant to what you want. It is wise to know the range of salaries commanded by those in the position that you seek, so that you can have a fact-based discussion of your expectations for compensation in the new job. Salary information is available. Many universities and schools of nursing maintain salary surveys of graduating classes that can provide guidelines for you. Web sites and professional journals provide salary information as well. Take a look at web sites that include salary information for health care careers (see Chapter 4).

Groundwork for Negotiation

You have laid positive groundwork with good interviews and warm feelings leading to a job offer. The employer hopes to hire you and has already committed time and energy to recruiting you.

Salary is one consideration. If the stated salary is less than you had hoped, but the job seems right for you and you wish to accept it, you may explain why you had expected more, what salary you had hoped to command and why, and express your hope that the salary offer is flexible. Some employers have flexibility and some do not; it is senseless to request more in salary if you have already been told that the salary is fixed.

After a positive interview and verbal offer, you are in a strong position to ask for what you want. Be reasonable and think about why an employer should pay you more. Your need for the money is not enough. The extraordinary value in education, experience, or skill that you bring is what constitutes grounds for reconsideration of a salary offer. Comparative data on salaries and equivalent responsibilities and job titles (which you have previously collected—see Chapter 4) is also very compelling.

Your starting salary is a significant consideration, since future salary increases are based on starting salary. A salary raise of 5 percent per year is a good solid increase, and 10 percent is highly unusual. Where you start makes a difference in the long run. If starting salary is lower than you had hoped, you may ask for an early salary review. It is to your advantage to start at a satisfactory salary, since future earnings will be based on it.

Once an employer is enthusiastic about hiring you, other points may be negotiable as well. You may wish to request a little more time to make your decision; take time to think about whether you wish to accept or decline a job offer. Once a job offer is made, employers often push you for a quick decision. If you need it, ask for more time to consider the offer. In so doing, you may be more certain that the decision is right for both of you. Requesting another week or two for decision-making is usually acceptable. If you are under consideration for another job that you might wish to take, contact that second employer to let them know of your need to make a decision.

Negotiating

Base your salary negotiation on what you learned in your research of the salary range for your particular field, your location, and your level of responsibility. Know the value of your contribution to a health care team. (For detailed information about calculating the value of a nurse practitioner to a clinical practice, refer to Carolyn Knight Buppert, JD, CRNP, "Negotiating Salary," *American Journal for Nurse Practitioners*, Fall 1997.) A seasoned professional who quickly assumes a great workload with little supervision and few consultations will contribute more to a practice than a new practitioner, for example.

After looking at the total compensation package for your job offer, determine if the offer is financially in line with your expectations and comparable data. If so, you may wish to add a few less essential considerations to your deliberation.

Conveniences like negotiating a starting date with a month off between school and your starting date may be discussed as well. If your plans do not fit with the employer's expectations, talk with the contact person and request a start date that works for you. It is important to demonstrate your willingness to be flexible when possible, but it is also appropriate for you to ask for what you want and proceed with your plans and dreams when realistic. Once offered the job, you may also wish to mention plans that you have already made, such as an upcoming special vacation or extra time to help the family adjust to a move.

The section below entitled "What to Consider in a Job Offer" is simply a list of ideas to keep in mind when considering a job offer. Determine what is most important to you. Make a list of the essential components, from your personal perspective, in a job offer. This should not be a long list, but pared down to be the necessary ingredients for your accepting the job. A second list may contain items that you would *like* to see in a job offer, but that are not required.

Think through your priorities and be prepared to present your thoughts to the employer concisely. You may wish to call the employer once to ask for answers to your questions and discuss your concerns. If certain issues or items on the list below are of great importance to you, say so.

Once you have your questions answered, sit down with the information and think through it. It is best not to continue to call with questions. Formulate your questions in advance and call the contact person when you have established priorities. If there is a benefits department and it is difficult to understand the literature about health care coverage, for example, that department or the insurance carrier should be able to answer detailed questions. It is best to avoid repeated calls to the contact person with questions about benefits.

Once you have made the decision to accept the job, accept in writing. Follow up in writing if you accept verbally. If you decide that the job is not the right fit for you, write a positive letter declining the offer. See "Sample Letters Accepting and Declining Offers" in Chapter 3. Again, remember that the professional team with whom you are dealing today may be your colleagues in the future.

Honor Your Decision to Accept a Job Offer

It is important to honor your word. Do not renege after accepting a job. Be certain that you evaluate a job offer thoughtfully and accept or decline based on careful consideration. Your professional reputation may depend on it.

What to Consider in a Job Offer

The suggestions offered below cover a wide range of possibilities. RNs working in inpatient facilities will probably have standard benefit packages, which do not allow much flexibility. In times of nursing shortages, however, new nurses may be offered special financial incentives. Some of the other considerations below will be most applicable to nurse practitioners and advanced practice nurses.

Benefits: Usually set in advance, benefits are important in your decision-making, as they may be very valuable. Full-time positions should include malpractice, life, worker's compensation, disability coverage, and health insurance for you and possibly for your family at varying costs. Be sure to ask if there is a waiting period before benefits begin.

Financial incentives: Especially during times of nursing shortages, nursing graduates may be encouraged to consider employers who offer extraordinary financial incentives. In addition to strong base salaries, RNs may be offered extra pay for agreeing to work during the least desirable hours or on shift differentials. Signing bonuses and bonuses for employees who stay with the employer for a certain period of time are also possibilities in times of shortage. In addition, some employers offer school loan repayment in exchange for a work commitment.

Vacation and other time off: Be clear about the vacation and sick-leave policies. Family leave, eldercare leave, maternity leave, or other personal time may be available to you if needed. After you are offered the job, you may wish to talk about vacation plans already in place. Perhaps you have a long-standing plan to take a two-week vacation shortly after you begin the new job. Get the plan on the table for discussion so you don't worry about it and the employer can plan for it.

Retirement: Learn what kind of retirement and/or savings plan, such as 401(k) or 403(b), is available with the employer and when you may begin to participate. Check to see if the employer contributes to the plan and at what level. Factor these into your salary calculations, as these are valuable financial considerations.

Location/travel time: Consider the costs and time associated with your commute. Inquire about public transportation possibilities, traffic patterns, and parking options. These factors play a role in the stress or comfort level you experience on the job.

Place: Get a feeling for the physical environment. Be sure that it is pleasant and safe. No doubt, you will spend many hours at the new workplace.

Relocation assistance: In some cases an employer will contribute to your moving expenses, advise spouses about opportunities, offer housing on a temporary or long-term basis, or provide home locator services. These factors could make a difference in the feasibility of relocating, or your willingness to move.

Educational support: Some employers reimburse tuition, such as master's programs to enhance the skills of their workforce. In this case, you may continue to work and receive a paycheck while earning an advanced degree or further education provided by your employer. This is a financial boost, as well as an investment in your future.

Professional development: Determine in what ways you will be able to grow professionally in the new workplace. Some employers arrange regularly scheduled exchanges of ideas among colleagues to promote professional development. Others provide funds to support your attendance at professional conferences in your specialty each year and allow time for courses that pertain to your patient population or discipline. Check to see about regular collaboration with colleagues on challenging cases. Be sure that your professional growth will be enhanced by the work experience.

Assignments/Requirements of position: Strive to get a true picture of what your working life will be like in the new job. Talk to the person who preceded you in the position if possible. Ask about the patient-to-nurse ratio or how many patients you will be expected to see in a day. Ask about the makeup of patient needs on your designated unit or about the most common presentations by patients. Check to see that the new environment is conducive to your good health.

Supervision/Consultation: An important criterion for accepting a job should be regular opportunity for productive supervision. Determine if you will have opportunity to learn from superior professional models or to enjoy excellent supervision and mentoring. Learn who will oversee your work and how you will get feedback. If you are an advanced practice nurse, you may want to know with whom you will consult on difficult issues, if there is a cost involved in consultation, and who pays it.

Evaluation and salary review: Inquire about the process of evaluating your performance. Ask who will provide the evaluation and how often you will be reviewed. Salary increases may be considered on an annual basis, sometimes linked to performance. Perhaps you would like to know about recent pay increases and if there is a standard or an exceptional salary increase possible.

Computer for home use: Doing paperwork while traveling or at home is facilitated by use of portable or home computers. If this may be an issue for you, ask about it.

Time commitment: Determine, in advance, what an employer's expectations are for your hours of service. Learn what shifts are available and the number of hours expected. Ask if overtime hours are voluntary or mandatory. For clinical nurse specialists or nurse practitioners it may be important to understand, in advance, if you will be depended upon to open the office every day at 8:00 A.M. or to know that this responsibility will be shared with a coworker. Determine the hours you will need to work to get the job done and what hours are customary for working in this role. Learn if you will be expected to assume on-call responsibilities. If it is important that you work at home occasionally to complete paperwork, ask if this will be possible.

Stock options: Occasionally, small start-up companies offer stock options in lieu of higher salaries. Stock options can be worthwhile if the company becomes profitable, they retain value, and you exercise them.

Additional perquisites: Consideration of these extra benefits may add value to your offer. Employers associated with educational institutions may offer educational financial support, not only for you, but also for your spouse or your children. This potential economic advantage should be considered when calculating overall compensation. Other perquisites may include amenities like health club memberships, convenient parking, cab or van services, cafeterias, break rooms, exercise rooms, nearby childcare at reasonable cost, or emergency childcare.

Contracts

High-level nursing professionals may be asked to sign an employment contract. Some advantages may ensue to the nursing professional through the use of a contract. The process of negotiating a contract allows you and your colleague or supervisor or manager to openly discuss and state the terms of your employment and the expectations on the part of each of you. The process opens a dialogue and clarifies potentially controversial issues and states these in writing so that the contract may be referred to when issues are disputed.

Some of the areas frequently covered in contracts are services expected from you, terms for on-call responsibilities, office hours expected and number of patients to be seen, bonuses, compensation, length of employment, reasons for termination, and restrictions on competition. A contract provides advantages for both the employee and the employer although most contracts are drafted by the employer's lawyer and are written for the employer's protection. Read every word of the contract carefully with your interests in mind. For example, if the employer requires that you give three months' notice before leaving, you may wish to ask that the employer write in a provision that allows you three months notice before your employment can be terminated, offering you an equivalent amount of protection. Ask an attorney who is experienced in employment law and with nurse practitioners' or physicians' contracts to review yours. Be careful to discuss fee structures with the attorney, in advance; you may be charged for research, telephone contact, and secretarial and copying services, in addition to face-to-face time. Carolyn Buppert's *Nurse Practitioner's Business Practice and Legal Guide* (Gaithersburg, Md.: Aspen Publishers, 1999) offers comprehensive information on contracts and lawyers' fees.

6
Creative Uses for Nursing and Health Care Backgrounds

Many nursing/health care professionals are prepared from the time they enter college, or even before, to serve in traditional roles that are based on economies and systems that no longer exist. It is challenging to keep your eyes trained on your goals and values in working on behalf of others and, at the same time, to consider the trends and realities of our current health care markets. As challenges in health care are met with innovative programs and technology, the skills needed to excel in traditional nursing and health care roles are becoming more complex and demanding. Change is inevitable and, when viewed as filled with possibilities, offers opportunity. Successful nursing and health care professionals will be lifelong learners, remaining flexible and adaptable; these professionals will be prepared for advancement throughout their careers.

In addition, many nurses work outside traditional health care settings, hold a wide variety of jobs and utilize nursing education and experience in nontraditional ways. Nursing and health care education, skill development, and experience offer a broad base of acquired abilities; nurses and other health care professionals often apply these skills to nontraditional settings.

Assess Your Skills

Regardless of your educational background and experience, every professional may profit from reassessing his or her personality, interests, and skills as transitions are considered. Some paper and pencil tests administered by trained professionals include the Myers-Briggs personality test and the Strong Interest Inventory. Some self-assessment tools available on the web are the Kiersey Temperament Sorter (www.keirsey.com) and The Career Key (www2.ncsu.edu/

unity/lockers/users/l/lkj). Print resources are numerous and include catchy titles like *Coming Alive from Nine to Five* by Betty Neville Michelozzi (Mayfield, 1996), *Do What You Are: Discover the Perfect Career By Personality Type,* by Paul Tieger (Lebanon, Ind.: Little, Brown, 1992), *What Color Is Your Parachute: Practical Manual for Job Hunters and Career Changers,* by Richard Nelson Bolles (Berkeley, Calif.: Ten Speed Press, 1999), and *Zen and the Art of Making a Living,* by Laurence G. Boldt (River Forest, Ill.: Planning/Communications, 1994). Self-assessment, setting of goals, and recognition of your gifts and talents may help you move toward work that stimulates and satisfies more fully.

Sometimes your needs will be met in traditional roles; at other times, less traditional positions may be the better match. Think expansively about what you have to offer and in what kind of setting you may find satisfaction.

Explore a Wide Range of Fields

The section below is designed to expand your horizons in contemplating and exploring possible career fields and job titles. These samples are simply ideas to stimulate your imagination. Job titles and requirements vary widely by organization. Listed below are some ideas for those considering alternative professional roles. In most instances, the job titles below would require experience in the field and education at the bachelor's or master's level.

Biotechnology and Pharmaceuticals

Job Titles: Sales representative; marketing associate; clinical research associate; quality assurance assistant; quality control specialist; product development specialist; medical monitor; director of clinical protocols.

Requirements: Experience in sales; product knowledge or development experience; experience or education in marketing; patient assessment and interviewing skills; research experience (pharmaceutical companies often hire clinical research organizations to perform clinical trials; these organizations also offer potential employment for nurses).

Resources: *Research Centers Directory,* edited by Donna Wood (Detroit: Gale, 1999); for health: *Care Industry Almanac,* by Jack Plunkett (Galveston, Tex.: Plunkett Research, 1995), the Riley Guide to pharmaceutical links (www.rileyguide.com/health.html pharm), the Biotechnology Directory (http://guide.nature.com/resfull.html); for pharmaceutical and biotechnology industry research (www.wetfeet. com/industries_co_asp), Medzilla (www.chemistry.com), Yahoo (http: //dir.yahoo.com/Business_and_Economy/Business_to_Business/ Health_Care/Pharmaceuticals/Directories/), and Pharmaceutical Careers (www.pharmaceuticalcareers.com).

College Administration and Student Services

Job Titles: Counselor; academic, career, or pre-health adviser; residence life supervisor; director of nursing admissions; development officer; health services nurse.

Requirements: Experience working with teens and young adults; advising, development, or managerial experience in higher education or a similar setting; interest in development of youth.

Resources: Chronicle of Higher Education, (www.chronicle.merit. edu), Higher Education Jobs On Line, (www.hire-ed.org) and (www. academic360.com); for positions in academia (www.job-hunt.org/aca demia.html); and for positions in student affairs (www.StudentAffairs. com/jobs/).

Communications

Job Titles: Marketing and sales representative; production or program assistant; editor; talk show host; health care columnist; health researcher in radio/TV; medical illustrator; technical writer/illustrator.

Requirements: Excellent presentation, writing, editing, and analytical skills; demonstration of abilities through samples of work; experience as an unpaid intern and paid work in area of specialty.

Resources: *Field Guide for Science Writers* edited by Blum and Knudson (Oxford and New York: Oxford University Press, 1997), *Hoover's Guide to Media Companies* (Austin, TX: Hoovers Business Press, 1996), *Opportunities in Television, Cable, Video and Multimedia* by Reed and Reed (Oxford and New York: Facts On File, 1999), and the Directory of Medical Publishers, (http://dir.yahoo.com/Business_and_Economy/Shopping_ and_Services/Publishers/Health/Medical_and_Professional/); for journalism and publishing industry research (www.wetfeet.com/asp/ industryprofiles_overview.osp?industrypk=23), the Biomedical Writers Association (www.amwa.org), and American Healthcare Publishing (www.amhpi.com). For information about freelance writing, take a look at http://freelancewrite.about.com/careers/freelancewrite/m body.htm and www.writersweekly.com.

Computing

Job Titles: Health information system trainee/trainer or consultant; informatics nurse specialist; information specialist; systems implementation specialist.

Requirements: Skill, experience, and interest in health-based technology and computing systems; informatics increasingly requires a highly trained person with a master's or PhD.

Resources: American Nursing Informatics Association (www.ania. org), Nursing Informatics Information (www.duke.edu/~mclen003/ medical.htm#Techno), the Health Information Management Systems Society (www.himss.org), and the National Association of Health Data Organizations (www.nahdo.org).

Consulting

Job Titles: Research analyst; health care staff consultant; health care analyst.

Requirements: Experience in research; analytical abilities; articulate, confident interpersonal style; knowledge of field in which consulting is required; orientation to business objectives.

Resources: *Harvard Business School Guide—Careers in Management Consulting* (Cambridge, MA: Harvard University Press, 1999), *Management Consulting: A complete Guide to the Industry* (Somerset, N.J.: John Wiley and Sons, 1999), *VGM Handbook of Business & Management Careers* by Criag T. Norback (Chicago: VGM Career Horizons, 1990), careers in consulting at www.ac.com/htm, consulting industry research at www. wetfeet.com/asp/industryprofiles_overview.asp?industrypk=12, www. vaultreports.com, or http://dir.yahoo.com/Business_and_Economy/ Business_to_Business/Health_Care/Consulting/.

Education

Job Titles: School of nursing faculty member; nursing school administrator; secondary school science/math teacher; preschool/elementary teacher; coach or trainer; special health programs teacher; counselor; drug and alcohol counselor; special programs administrator; science museum educator; school teen hotline facilitator.

Requirements: Certification is required for public school teachers; private schools do not require certification of teachers (science and math positions are often difficult to fill); experience in teaching and interest in particular educational program or setting; experience in developing and implementing programs; experience or education in area of specialty. Schools of nursing sometimes hire master's prepared nurses with clinical or teaching experience as faculty members.

Resources: *Alternative Teacher Certification: A State by State Analysis* by Emily Feinstritzer and David T. Chester (Washington, D.C.: National Center for Educational Information, 2000), the Academic Employment Network/Certification Information By State (www.academploy.com/certif.cfm), the American School Directory (www.asd.com), the Alpha List of Independent Boarding School Web Sites (www.schools.com/directory/alpha.html), the National Association of Independent Schools (www.nais.org), and the Chronicle of Higher Education (http://chronicle.merit.edu/free/jobs/faculty/scitech/links.htm).

Entrepreneurial

Job Titles: Geriatric program designer; vice president; owner; founder; create your own title.

Requirements: Creative ideas to meet specific marketable needs; ability to identify funding sources; ability to dream, identify a marketable product, and implement a plan; experience in business development, finance and personnel management; willingness to assume risk.

Resources: *Entrepreneuring: A Nurse's Guide to Starting a Business*, Gerry Vogel and Nancy Doleysh (National League of Nursing; New York: Jones and Bartlett, 1994), *Making It on Your Own* (Washington, Mo.: Paperbacks for Educators, 1991), *Homemade Money* by Barbara Brabec (Cincinnati, Oh.: Betterway Books, 1994); for career advice on entrepreneurship, www.vaultreports.com and http://careers.yahoo.com/.

Government

Job Titles: Prison health nurse; Medicaid/Medicare program adviser; Peace Corps volunteer; political adviser.

Requirements: Patience and persistence in following formal guidelines; every level of government (federal, state, local) has specific procedures for applying; inquire about particular procedures for your area; some jobs require testing.

Resources: *The Government Job Finder*, by Daniel Lauber (River Forest, Ill.: Planning/Communications, 2000), Jobs in Government (http://jobsingovernment.com), USA Jobs from the Office of Personnel Management (http://usajobs.opm.gov), Government Jobs Central (http://federaljobs.net); and State Department (www.careers.state.gov).

Human Resources/Personnel

Job Titles: Training specialist; employee assistance health educator/ nurse; nurse recruiter; benefits administrator.

Requirements: Experience in human resources or special knowledge of area for training or recruiting; knowledge or interest in benefits, compensation, labor relations, or equal employment opportunities.

Resources: For human resources industry research (www.tcm.com/ hr-careers/career), the Society for Human Resource Management (www.shrm.org), the Training Supersite (www.trainingsupersite.com), the American Society for Training and Development (www.astd.org), and the International Association of Facilitators (www.iaf-world.org/ iaflinks.htm).

Human/Social Services

Job Titles: Project developer; community organizer; program director; outreach coordinator; counselor.

Requirements: Strong organizational skills and experience; ability to describe and demonstrate specific abilities and experience that relate to special project, community or clientele; professional, as well as, volunteer efforts are valued.

Resources: *The Non Profit and Education Job Finder* by Daniel Lauber (River Forest, Ill.: Planning/Communications, 1997), links to sites of 14,000 nonprofit organizations (www.idealist.org), Opportunity Nocs (www.opportunitynocs.com), The Foundation Center (www.fdn center.org), and Interglobal Non Profits (http://interglobal.com/inter global/content/nonprofit/index.html).

Insurance

Job Titles: Disability management nurse, claims representative or examiner; underwriter; medical claims preapproval contact; group sales representative.

Requirements: Experience or coursework in case management; attention to detail; analytical and evaluative abilities; strong interpersonal skills; familiarity with the insurance industry.

Resources: Insurance Career Center (http://connectyou.com/ talent/), Insurance Overview (www.careers-in-finance.com/in.htm), Yahoo insurance recruiting links (http://dir.yahoo.com/Business_and _Economy/Business_to_Business/Corporate_Services/Human_Re sources/Recruiting_and_Placement/Career-Fields/Insurance), and insurance industry research (www.wetfeet.com/asp/industryprofiles_overview.asp?Industry_pk=20).

Law and Law Enforcement

Job Titles: Legal nurse consultant; legal researcher; litigation support consultant; forensics nurse; hospital general counsel; medical patent lawyer; regulatory expert.

Requirements: Experience in research and analysis; interest in assisting attorneys, insurance companies, and health care institutions with legal issues related to medical practices; experience or interest in combining clinical practice with law enforcement. For counsel and regulatory positions, a law degree and experience in the health care or regulatory environment are essential.

Resources: *Directories of Expert Witnesses and Consultants* (Washington, D.C.: Legal Times—a series of regional directories from the American Lawyer Media, LP), *What Can you Do With a Law Degree* by Deborah Arron (River Forest, Ill.: Planning/Communications, 1997), American Association of Legal Nurse Consultants (www.aalnc.org), American Association of Nurse Attorneys (www.taana.org), Medical-Legal Consulting Institute, Inc.—education and CLNC certification (www.legalnurse.com), Forensic Nursing Education (www.forensiceducation.com/index1.htm), American Forensic Nurse Association (www.amrn.com), and International Association of Forensic Nurses (www.forensicnurse.org).

Market Research/Health Policy Research

Job Titles: Research assistant/associate; market researcher; health systems analyst; project manager.

Requirements: Interest in analyzing statistical data to determine market conditions; research and data analysis experience; interest and ability in preparation of written and verbal presentation of findings.

Resources: Health Groups in Washington—D.C.-based advocacy and policy groups (Washington, D.C.: National Health Council, 1999), International Directory of Marketing Research Companies and Services (American Marketing Association, 1999); for industry research on Marketing (www.vaultreports.com), Market Research Overview (www.careers-in-marketing.com/mr.htm), the Market Research Association (www.mra-net.org); and links to think tanks and other policy research resources (www.nira.go.jp/linke/tt-link/index.html).

Public Relations

Job Titles: Hospital public affairs director; public information specialist; press liaison; special events coordinator; community affairs liaison; patient relations director; publications editor.

Requirements: Writing and organizational ability; experience in promoting a favorable image for an institution or organization; experience in developing and implementing programs and activities that create favorable publicity.

Resources: *Public Relations Career Directory,* by Bradley J. Morgan, *Career Opportunities in Advertising and Public Relations* by Shelly Field (New York: Facts on File, 1996), *O'Dwyer's Directory of Public Relations Firms* (New York: O'Dwyer, 1999), *O'Dwyer's Directory of Corporate Communications* (New York: O'Dwyer, 1999), and National Directory of Corporate Public Affairs; for industry research (www.vaultreports.com) and (www.prfirms.org).

The fields, job titles, and qualifications above are designed to inspire creative thinking about new areas to explore. Every organization has its own educational and background requirements to meet their own unique needs. A selection to pique your interest, the information above does not represent a complete picture of professional fields, job titles, or requirements.

If you are interested in changing fields, contact alumni from your university and begin to talk with others about your new area of interest. Develop your new network for information and assistance. To explore career descriptions and information, take a look at www.wetfeet.com/asp/home.asp and www.vaultreports.com for industry specific research.

Your BSN and MSN colleagues have job titles like these actual job titles gathered from nursing school records of recent graduates.

Addictions nurse
Administrator
Admissions director
Advanced practice nurse
Ambulatory care coordinator
Analyst
Assessment specialist
Assistant division manager
Cardiology nurse
Care team coordinator
Certified nurse practitioner

Charge nurse
Clinical affairs consultant
Clinical coordinator
Clinical nurse specialist
Community health center nurse
Coordinator of practice activities
Corporate finance analyst
Course coordinator
Diabetes educator
Director of mayor's office of
    Medicaid

Director of wellness center
Discharge planner
Emergency room nurse
Environmental risk assessment
  officer
Executive search counselor
Family counselor
Family nurse practitioner
Financial aid advisor for health
  profession(s)
Financial analyst, health care
  division
Forensic nurse
Flight nurse
Geriatric nurse practitioner
Head nurse
Health educator
Health care consultant/
  liaison/rep
Holistic nurse
Home care director/liaison
Hospice nurse
Incontinence specialist
Infant development specialist
Infection control nurse
Instructor
Labor organizer
Lactation consultant
Long-term care coordinator
Medical abstractionist
Medical affairs coordinator
Navy officer
Nurse anesthetist
Nurse consultant
Nurse epidemiology interviewer
Nurse manager
Nurse midwife
Nurse psychotherapist
Nurse recruiter
Nurse supervisor
Nursing director

Nursing home administrator
Nutrition consultant
Obstetrics and gynecology nurse
Occupational health nurse
Office nurse
Oncology nurse
Operating room nurse
Pain manager
Parish nurse
Pediatric nurse
Perinatal nurse
Physician liaison
Policy project assistant
Pre-admission anesthesia
  evaluator
Project assistant/
  coordinator/manager
Public health nurse
Referral coordinator
Rehabilitation nurse
Resident nurse
School nurse
Science educator at
  museums/library/school
Senior consultant
Short-stay clinical coordinator
Study coordinator
Sub-investigator
Supervisor
Surgical float nurse
Technical sales representative
Telephone triage nurse
Transplant coordinator
Trauma prevention coordinator
Traveling nurse
Union organizer
University health systems nurse
University relations officer
Veterinary nurse
Visiting nurse

Tap into your imagination and you can add titles of your own to the list. Nursing education and experience can be a solid foundation for a wide variety of educational programs and professions. Additional skills may come naturally, expressed through volunteerism, cultivated in current employment settings, or gained through education and internships.

A True Story: Nursing to Finance

Possible role models for nurses who have successfully navigated career changes are many. One career-change evolution captured my attention: June A. Schroeder continuously assessed her skills, explored nontraditional roles, and took risks to find personal satisfaction.

June A. Schroeder is president and shareholder of Liberty Financial Group in Elm Grove, Wisconsin. She also has her own radio show and appears as a guest on television. June began her career as a nurse.

Perhaps surprisingly, many skills from her nursing education and experience are applicable to her current career as a financial planner. In my conversations with June, she shared some insight about her personal and professional philosophy as well as the transitions in her work history.

Hard work has been an essential part of June's work and personal life. While she was a high school student, June's father died, and she sought the support of adult mentors in her school life. She worked in a variety of jobs to save money and managed to acquire financial support to allow for a college education. As a full-time BSN student at the University of Wisconsin in Milwaukee, June worked several jobs, including medical transcriber, waitress, and theater ticket salesperson, to make ends meet. Following graduation, she volunteered for the summer with the student health organization, doing what was called medical social work for welfare recipients in 1969 during the unrest around the Vietnam War. Her first paid position after graduation was working second shift at a Veterans' Administration hospital in neurosurgery. In this role, June volunteered to organize the maze of nurses' schedules for her wing of the hospital. Even then, she assumed challenges and demonstrated and explored her interest in organizing and bringing together the pieces of a puzzle.

Since she enjoyed working with older adults, June became a supervisor in a rehabilitation nursing home. Even though she was performing work she enjoyed and felt very good at it, she described experiencing a "slightly discordant note." She had a feeling that something else was a better fit for her.

An advertisement in the local paper for a director of economic security for the Wisconsin Nursing Association caught June's eye. She did not know exactly what the job entailed, but she was attracted by the title since she believed that all nurses should have economic security. Impressed with the thought, June organized her own financial affairs, bought a house, took an adventurous trip to Europe, applied for the job, and got it. In retrospect, she believes that she was chosen for the position for her potential as a leader. Most likely, June exuded enthusiasm and interest, demonstrated a strong work ethic and organizational skills through work history and recommendations, and presented herself articulately.

As director of economic security, faced with stacks of administrative documents like the Taft-Hartley Act, June welcomed the challenge and studied ferociously. In this role, June was called upon to utilize skills as yet untapped. At twenty-five years of age, she had assumed union leadership, speaking before crowded rooms of people, negotiating contracts, and addressing grievances. She expressed her interest in quantitative issues and education by learning about member benefits and financial packages. June demonstrated her ongoing belief that trying new things by "being gutsy when you are shivering inside" is a winning strategy.

June served in her role with the Wisconsin Nursing Association for seven years and sought something more. With encouragement from supervisors and mentors, she began study toward a master's degree in Milwaukee. She pursued coursework for about two years. Even though she was strongly supported by faculty members in her independent master's work in nursing, June continued to feel that her full array of talents were not being used.

June attended a financial seminar for women. Impressed with the information, she began her study of financial planning. June knew she had found her calling, and licensure in financial services was her next goal. True to herself, June developed her own business, which was first housed in her living room, and worked hard to make it succeed. She has developed such a following in the field of personal and business financial planning that she hosts her own radio show and appears as a TV guest. June writes articles that appear in various publications including Nursingmatters, a Wisconsin-based newspaper for RNs. She has also contracted with CNBC.com to write articles for their website. This provides her with a forum through which she can constantly emphasize her belief that money is a health issue—that financial stress, one of our biggest stresses today, can make you sick.

June A. Schroeder's Prescriptions for Nurses in Transition

"Check the label three times." Invest in learning about yourself; investigate options and gather facts. Confirm that information and your interpretation of the facts are accurate. June always checks to see that she understands her client correctly. She does not rely on assumptions or her own experience but on focused listening and confirmation of facts. Both in her nursing and her financial advising roles, acquiring accurate information is the only way to be assured that she provides good advice and creates appropriate care plans. This applies to you and to those with whom you interact.

Assume responsibility for creative and individual approaches and solutions. Each person has a different personality, history, and varied set of skills and needs. June relies on not only her accuracy, but also on her independent thought, innovative ideas, and problem-solving abilities to help address client needs as well as her own.

Invest in people. Get to know those around you, ask them about themselves, demonstrate your enthusiasm for the roles you play, develop mentors, and mentor others. People with whom you interact often reappear in your life. Patients, seatmates, colleagues, as well as supervisors, may affect your life at some time in the future. Invest in what you are doing and in those with whom you interact. June met a man on an airplane who was the CEO of a company. As a result of their becoming acquainted on the trip, he provided valuable business advice and counsel over a period of years.

"Put one foot in front of the other." In times of hardship, June relied on this simple rule. She has an optimistic attitude, which has carried her over in times of personal or business trouble. Do all that you can and keep your eyes focused on your goals. "Opportunity does not come along every day . . . take the challenge and stretch yourself."

Honor your special talents and gifts. Whether you pursue your talents in your professional life or as an avocation, it is important to "be true to yourself." From the time she was a young girl, June loved math and science. She enjoyed puzzles and other forms of problem-solving. Each choice along her career path has utilized another aspect of her innate ability. Each time she stretched herself and accepted a challenge, she added something significant to her repertoire of skills.

7
Advanced Nursing Education

Many talented nursing professionals today are graduates of hospital-based diploma programs; with intelligence, dedication, experience, and ongoing education, you successfully address patient needs on a daily basis. As health care becomes more sophisticated, however, demand for broadly educated and clinically experienced nurses will only grow greater. Hospitals will continue to become more technologically based, used for critical and emergency care, unusual diagnoses requiring special care, and medical research. Outpatient, home care, and long-term care facilities will receive more acute or subacute care patients, demanding greater skills of the nurses who serve in these settings. The most highly valued nursing professionals, requiring higher pay, will have, at least, a bachelor of science (BS or BSN) degree.

Baccalaureate nursing programs offer students a well-rounded education. Enriched by liberal arts coursework and exposed to multidisciplinary approaches, which stimulate critical thinking, BSN graduates have an opportunity to gain mature and critical approaches to problem solving as well as to develop effective communication skills. The combination of liberal arts and science education coupled with clinical experience is a winning formula for the individual as well as for the future of health care. In addition to the intrinsic value of a broad background, increasing use of technology and the level of sophistication of care in many medical facilities require more nurses educated at the baccalaureate and master's levels. Registered nurses will be expected to handle an increasingly demanding level of practice. The Health Resources and Services Administration recently wrote that the expanding role of registered nurses "requires critical thinking and problem solving skills; a sound foundation in a broad range of basic sciences, knowledge of behavioral, social and management sciences; and the ability to communicate and analyze. . . . Baccalaureate education provides a base from which nurses move into graduate education to fulfill the expanding needs for nurses in advanced practice and management of complex health care systems." The broad-based education and clinical experiences that accompany the bachelor of science in nursing degrees prepare tomorrow's nursing professionals for the wide-ranging challenges of the future. The BSN degree is the entry-level degree for nurses who wish to contribute eventually at the highest professional levels.

The BSN degree, coupled with nursing work experience, is also a strong foundation for higher-level specialty preparation. Some employers will provide specialized skill-based education through in-house programs, which may include skill development, as well as mentoring and experience in the specialty. Other nurses who want to be adaptable and take advantage of advanced nursing opportunities will pursue graduate programs. To determine what programs may be appropriate for your needs, check with the American Association of Colleges of Nursing at www.aacn.nche.edu/education/Resindex.htm.

Master's programs prepare practitioners to contribute in even more specialized roles. In support of advanced nursing education, AACN President Andrea R. Lindell, DNSc, RN, writes "As policymakers work to control costs and give Americans wider access to affordable, basic health care, planners are turning more to nurse practitioners—advanced registered nurses with primary-care and acute-care skills—to deliver high quality, front-line health services in an array of settings throughout the community." Master's prepared nurses will fill a wide range of professional roles. NONPF President, Christine Boodley, PhD, RN, FNP, writes, "Nurse practitioners have the ability to fill emerging roles in the health care marketplace, with graduates exhibiting increased flexibility by the range of specialties they enter. As predicted in the early days of the profession, the nurse practitioner role spans a wide variety of settings."

Those who wish to assume leadership in the field of nursing will probably have a master's degree. Those who wish to pursue careers in other fields based on their nursing education and experience may need to pursue additional coursework or degrees. Check with professionals in your field of interest to determine if business, finance, organizational, computing, education coursework, or additional degrees may increase your chances of moving smoothly to your preferred job.

Finance Your Education

Further education is a powerful professional advantage, yet financing it may seem overwhelming. Go forward on the assumption that financing is available and scout for it.

Schools of nursing are the first place to ask about financial assistance opportunities; educational institutions are motivated to be of assistance since they hope that strong candidates will enroll in their nursing programs. Some candidates earn assistance through need. Others receive funding through special programs or for their accomplishments. The American Association of Colleges of Nursing and other nursing organizations endorsed an increase in 1999 for funding for education of baccalaureate and advanced practice nurses through the Nurse Education Act. Federal loans appropriated annually by Congress, are available on a need basis, and those seeking nursing education may qualify for a student loan.

There are many resources for scholarships and loans. Professional associations often provide financial support to encourage others to enter their field or specialty. Some examples are the Association for Gerontology in Higher Education (www.aghe.org/UGbroint.htm), the American Association of Critical Care Nurses (www.aacn.org), the Neuroscience Nursing Foundation (www.aann.org), and the National Association of Hispanic Nurses (www.hsf.net/). Inquire with national nursing organizations with which you have an affinity.

Scholarship and loan forgiveness opportunities are also available through regional resources. The Hope Scholarship supports Georgia residents, who graduate from high school with a B average, at any college or university in the state. Pennsylvania offers loan forgiveness and scholarship funds to nursing candidates to cover some of the costs of a nursing education. For more resources on financial aid refer to the *Guide to Nursing Programs* (Lawrenceville, N.J.: Peterson's Guides, 1999) and visit *Nursing Spectrum*'s section on scholarships and grants at www.nursingwebsearch.com, as well as www.grantsbiz.com and www.grantsnet.org/.

Employers are well served by encouraging skill advancement and educational attainment in their nursing staff. Ask your current employer about opportunities for tuition reimbursement, in-service training, or long-distance learning. Scholarships from potential employers sometimes offer funding or loan forgiveness to junior and senior nursing students in exchange for paid service in their medical center following graduation.

The U.S. government provides avenues for financial assistance and education. The Reserve Officer Training Corps supports undergraduates in exchange for service in the Army Nurse, Navy Nurse and Air Force Nursing Corps. The United States Department of Health and Human Service also offers scholarships (www.os.dhhs.gov) and grants (www.hhs.gov/grantsnet) for baccalaureate, master's, and doctoral preparation.

In addition, the U.S. government encourages a redistribution of health services to underserved domestic communities with educational incentives for those with a spirit for service and adventure. The National Health Service Corps (www.bphc.hrsa.gov/nhsc or call 800-221-9393) offers traineeships, scholarships, and loan repayment programs. Under the same organizational umbrella are other programs that offer financial incentives for schoolwork in conjunction with valuable service. Two of these are the Indian Health Service, through which nurses work in Native American communities, and the Northwest Regional Primary Care Association (www.nwrpca.org/), through which nurse practitioners serve in Alaska, Idaho, Oregon, and Washington. Teach for America (1-800-TEA-1230) offers deferral or cancellation of certain student loans as well as tuition assistance for future graduate study and is an option for both baccalaureate and advanced practice nurses.

International health care through the Peace Corps (www.peacecorps.gov or 1-800-424-8580) also offers some financial remuneration for education to those who wish to serve and explore other cultures. Some portion of your student loans may be deferred or canceled while you serve in the Peace Corps.

Experience is the calling card for nurses in advanced degree programs. A couple of years of work as an RN provide a strong basis for fully appreciating further nursing education or advanced practice degrees. Many nurses who return to school, as well as students entering nursing schools for the first time, work in the profession while studying. The rigor of part-time work or ongoing nursing service while continuing your education at an advanced level is a challenge worth taking on. Gain as much experience as possible before you market yourself as an advanced practice nurse or nurse practitioner. Your confidence will grow and you will be prepared to contribute at the level that your accomplishments and degrees warrant.

If you are a returning student, the depth of experience that you bring to the job search, combined with your high-level academic program experiences, offers a tremendous opportunity. You have colleagues who know you and supervisors who see the daily quality of your work; add to the powerful mix the relationships being developed with advanced practice faculty members and future colleagues within your educational program. The rigorous routines, which may be exhausting some days, may also create a formula for success. Opportunity to show your best colors is available to you at two professional levels.

Students and professionals demonstrate abilities by having accomplished a task or used particular skills in a class, a workplace, or another setting. If you hope to transfer your skills to a different type of employer, enter a new workplace, utilize a new set of skills, or demonstrate abilities, you'll need experience. Courses of study, assignments for class, projects for faculty, as well as work assignments, work projects, volunteer projects, and hobbies are all ways to gain the experience that may translate to skill-building for an employer.

ADVANCED PRACTICE TITLES

Nurse Practitioner

Clinical Nurse Specialist

Certified Nurse Midwife

Certified Registered Nurse Anesthetist

MASTER'S PROGRAM CONCENTRATIONS

Acute/Tertiary/Chronic Care Nursing

Adult/Gerontological Health Nursing

Case Management

Clinical Nurse Specialist

Community/Public Health Nursing

Critical Care Nursing

Emergency Nursing

Family Health Nursing

Home Health Nursing

Maternity-Newborn Nursing

Medical-Surgical Nursing

Neonatal Health

Nurse Midwife

Nursing Administration

Nursing Education

Nursing Informatics

Occupational Health Nursing

Oncology Nursing

Parent-Child Nursing

Pediatric Acute/Chronic/ Critical Care Nursing

Primary Care Nurse Practitioner

Psychiatric/Mental Health Nursing

Rehabilitation Nursing

School Health

Women's Health

A master's degree and/or specialized training is required for these disciplines. For information on academic programs, contact the American Association of Colleges of Nursing at www.aacn.nche.edu/education/Resindex.htm.

Appendix 1
State Licensing Boards

National Council of State Boards of Nursing
www.ncsbn.org

Alabama Board of Nursing
P.O. Box 303900
Montgomery, AL 36130-3900
(334) 242-4060/ Fax: (334) 242-4360
www.abn.state.al.us/

Alaska Board of Nursing
Department of Community and Economic Development
Division of Occupational Licensing
P.O. Box 110806
Anchorage, AK 99811-0806
(907) 269-8161 or 465-2544/ Fax: (907) 465-2974
www.dced.state.ak.us/occ/pnur.htm

Arizona State Board of Nursing
1651 East Morten Avenue, Suite 150
Phoenix, AZ 85020
(602) 331-8111/ Fax: (602) 906-9365
www.azboardofnursing.org/

Arkansas State Board of Nursing
University Tower Building
1123 South University Avenue, Suite 800
Little Rock, AR 72204-1619
(501) 686-2700/ Fax: (501) 686-2714
www.state.ar.us/nurse

California Board of Registered Nursing
400 R. Street, Suite 4030
P.O. Box 944210
Sacramento, CA 95814
(916) 322-3350/ Fax: (916) 327-4402
www.rn.ca.gov/

Colorado Board of Nursing
1560 Broadway, Suite 670
Denver, CO 80202
(303) 894-2430/ Fax: (303) 894-2821
www.dora.state.co.us/Nursing/

Connecticut Board of Examiners for Nursing
Div. of Health Systems Regulation
410 Capital Avenue, MS#12HSR
P.O. Box 340308
Hartford, CT 06134-0308
(860) 509-8000/ Fax: (860) 509-7295
www.state.ct.us/dph/

Delaware Board of Nursing
861 Silver Lake Boulevard
Cannon Building, Suite 203
P.O. Box 1401
Dover, DE 19904
(302) 739-4522/ Fax: (302) 739-2711

District of Columbia Board of Nursing
614 H Street, NW, Room 904
Washington, DC 20001
(202) 442-4778/ Fax: (202) 442-9431

Florida Board of Nursing
4080 Woodcock Drive, Suite 202
Jacksonville, FL 32207-2714
(850) 488-0595
www.doh.state.fl.us/mqa/nursing/nur_home.html

Georgia Board of Nursing
166 Pryor Street, SW
Atlanta, GA 30303-3465

(478) 207-1640/ Fax: (478) 207-1660
www.sos.state.ga.us/plb/rn/

Hawaii Board of Nursing
Department of Commerce and Consumer Affairs
P.O. Box 3469
Honolulu, HI 96801
(808) 586-2695/ Fax: (808) 586-2689
www.state.hi.us/dcca/pvl/areas_nurse.html

Idaho Board of Nursing
280 North 8th Street, Suite 210
P.O. Box 83720
Boise, ID 83720-0061
(208) 334-3110/ Fax: (208) 334-3262
www2.state.id.us/ibn/ibnhome.htm

Illinois Department of Professional Regulation
James R. Thompson Center
100 West Randolph, Suite 9-300
Chicago, IL 60601
(312) 814-2715/ Fax: (312) 814-1837
www.dpr.state.il.us/

Indiana State Board of Nursing
Health Professions Bureau
402 West Washington Street, Suite 041
Indianapolis, IN 46204
(317) 232-2960/ Fax: (317) 233-4236
www.state.in.us/hpb/boards/isbn/

Iowa Board of Nursing
State Capitol Complex
1223 East Court Avenue
Des Moines, IA 50319
(515) 281-3255/ Fax: (515) 281-4825
www.state.ia.us/government/nursing/

Kansas State Board of Nursing
Landon State Office Building
900 SW Jackson, Suite 551-S
Topeka, KS 66612

(785) 296-4929/ Fax: (785) 296-3929
www.ksbn.org

Kentucky Board of Nursing
312 Whittington Parkway Suite 300
Louisville, KY 40222
(502) 329-7000/ Fax: (502) 329-7011
www.kbn.state.ky.us/

Louisiana State Board of Nursing
3510 North Causeway Boulevard, Suite 501
Metairie, LA 70002
(504) 838-5332/ Fax: (504) 838-5349
www.lsbn.state.la.us/

Maine State Board of Nursing
158 State House Station
Augusta, ME 04333
(207) 287-1133/ Fax: (207) 287-1149
www.state.me.us/nursingbd/

Maryland Board of Nursing
4140 Patterson Avenue
Baltimore, MD 21215
(410) 585-1900/ Fax: (410) 358-3530
www.mbon.org/

Massachusetts Board of Registration in Nursing
Leverett Saltonstall Building
239 Causeway Street
Boston, MA 02114
(617) 727-9961/ Fax: (617) 727-2197
www.state.ma.us/reg/boards/rn/

Michigan Board of Nursing
CIS/Office of Health Services
Ottawa Towers North
611 West Ottawa, 4th Floor
Lansing, MI 48933
(517) 373-9102/ Fax: (517) 373-2179
www.cis.state.mi.us/bhser/genover.htm

Minnesota Board of Nursing
2829 University Avenue SE,
Suite 500
Minneapolis, MN 55414
(614) 617-2270/ Fax: (612) 617-2190
www.nursingboard.state.mn.us/

Mississippi Board of Nursing
1935 Lakeland Drive, Suite B
Jackson, MS 39216
(601) 987-4188/ Fax: (601) 364-2352
www.msbn.state.ms.us/

Missouri State Board of Nursing
3605 Missouri Boulevard
P.O. Box 656
Jefferson City, MO 65102
(573) 751-0681/ Fax: (573) 751-0075
www.ecodev.state.mo.us/pr/nursing/

Montana State Board of Nursing
P.O. Box 200513
Helena, MT 59620-0531
(406) 841-2340/ Fax: (406) 841-2343
www.discoveringmontana.com/dir/bsd/license/bsd_boards/num_
board/board_page.htm

Nebraska Department of Health and Human Services
Regulation & Licensure/Credentialing Division
Nursing/Nursing Support Section
P.O. Box 95007
Lincoln, NE 68509-5007
(402) 471-4376/ Fax: (402) 471-1066
www.hhs.state.ne.us/crl/nns.htm

Nevada State Board of Nursing
1755 East Plumb Lane, Suite 260
Reno, NV 89502
(775) 688-2620/ Fax: (775) 688-2628
www.nursingboard.state.nv.us

New Hampshire Board of Nursing
Health and Welfare Building
6 Hazen Drive
Concord, NH 03301
(603) 271-6599/ Fax: (603) 271-6605
www.state.nh.us/nursing/

New Jersey Board of Nursing
P.O. Box 45010
Newark, NJ 07101
(973) 504-6430/ Fax: (973) 648-3481
www.state.nj.us/lps/ca/medical.htm

New Mexico Board of Nursing
4206 Louisiana Boulevard NE, Suite A
Albuquerque, NM 87109
(505) 841-8340/ Fax: (505) 841-8347
www.state.nm.us/clients/nursing

New York State Board of Nursing
State Education Department
Cultural Education Center, Room 3023
Albany, NY 12230
(518) 474-3845/ Fax: 474-3706
www.nysed.gov/prof/nurse.htm

North Carolina Board of Nursing
P.O. Box 2129
Raleigh, NC 27602-2129
(919) 782-3211/ Fax: (919) 781-9461
www.ncbon.com/

North Dakota Board of Nursing
919 South 7th Street, Suite 504
Bismarck, ND 58504-5881
(701) 328-9778/ Fax: (701) 328-9785
www.ndbon.org/

Ohio Board of Nursing
77 South High Street, 17th Floor
Columbus, OH 43266
(614) 466-3947/ Fax: (614) 466-0388
www.state.oh.us/nur/

Oklahoma Board of Nursing
2915 North Classen Boulevard, Suite 524
Oklahoma City, OK 73106
(405) 962-1800/ Fax: (405) 962-1821

Oregon State Board of Nursing
800 NE Oregon Street, Box: 25
Suite 465
Portland, OR 97232-2162
(503) 731-4745/ Fax: (503) 731-4755
www.osbn.state.or.us/

Pennsylvania State Board of Nursing
P.O. Box 2649
Harrisburg, PA 17105-2649
(717) 783-7142/ Fax: (717) 783-0822
www.dos.state.pa.us/bpoa/nurbd/mainpage.htm

Commonwealth of Puerto Rico Board of Nurse Examiners
Box 10200
Santurce, PR 00908
(787) 725-8161/ Fax: (787) 725-7903

Rhode Island Board of Nurse Registration and Nursing Education
Cannon Health Building
Three Capitol Hill, Room 104
Providence, RI 02908
(401) 222-5700/ Fax: (401) 222-3352
www.health.state.ri.us

South Carolina State Board of Nursing
Kingstree Building, Synergy Business Park
Suite 202, P.O. Box 12367
110 Centerview Drive
Columbia, SC 29210
(803) 896-4550/ Fax: (803) 896-4525
www.llr.state.SC.US/POL/Nursing/

South Dakota Board of Nursing
3307 South Lincoln Avenue
Sioux Falls, SD 57105
(605) 362-2760/ Fax: (605) 362-2768
www.state.sd.us/dcr/nursing/

Tennessee State Board of Nursing
426 Fifth Avenue North, 1st Floor
Cordell Hull Building
Nashville, TN 37247
(615) 532-5166/ Fax: (615) 741-7899
www.state.tn.us/

Texas Board of Nurse Examiners
P.O. Box 430
Austin, TX 78767-0430
(512) 305-7400/ Fax: (512) 305-7401
www.bne.state.tx.us/

Utah State Board of Nursing
Div. of Occupational and Professional Licensing
Salt Lake City, UT 84145
(801) 530-6628
(801) 530-6511
www.commerce.state.ut.us/

Vermont State Board of Nursing
109 State Street
Montpelier, VT 05609-1101
(802) 828-2396/ Fax: (802) 828-2484
www.vtprofessionals.org/nurses/

Virgin Islands Board of Nurse Licensure
Veterans Drive Station
St. Thomas, VI 00803
(340) 776-7397/ Fax: (340) 777-4003

Virginia Board of Nursing
6606 West Broad Street, 4th Floor
Richmond, VA 23230-1717
(804) 662-9909/ Fax: (804) 662-9512
www.dhp.state.va.us/

Washington State Nursing Care Quality Assurance Commission
Dept. of Health, Box 47864
1300 SE Quince Street
Olympia, WA 98504-7864
(360) 236-4740/ Fax: (360) 236-4738
www.doh.wa.gov/nursing/

West Virginia State Board of Examiners for
Registered Professional Nurses
101 Dee Drive
Charleston, WV 25311-1620
(304) 558-3596/ Fax: (304) 558-3666
www.state.wv.us/nurses/rn/

Wisconsin Department of Regulation and Licensing
Bureau of Health Service Professions
P.O. Box 8935
Madison, WI 53708-8935
(608) 266-0145/ Fax: (608) 261-7083
www.wisconsin.gov/state/home

Wyoming State Board of Nursing
2020 Carey Avenue, Suite 110
Cheyenne, WY 82002
(307) 777-7601/ Fax: (307) 777-3519
www.nursing.state.wy.us/

Appendix 2
Credentialing Organizations

American Academy of Nursing Practitioners Certification Program
Capitol Station
P.O. Box 12926
Austin, TX 78711
(512) 442-5202
www.aanp.org

American Academy of Wound Management
1720 Kennedy Causeway, Suite 109
North Bay Village, FL 33141
(305) 866-9592
www.aawm.org
(CWS)

**American Association of Critical Care Nurses
Certification Corporation** (AACN)
101 Columbia
Aliso Viejo, CA 92656-1491
(949) 362-2000
www.aacn.org
certcorp@aacn.org

American Association of Nurse Anesthetists
222 South Prospect Avenue
Park Ridge, IL 60068-5790
(847) 692-7050
www.aana.com

American Board for Occupational Health Nurses
201 East Ogden, Suite 114

Hinsdale, IL 60521-3652
(888) 842-2646 or (630) 789-5799/ Fax: (630) 789-8901
www.abohn.org
(COHN, COHN-S)

**American Board of Neuroscience Nursing Professional
Examination Service**
4700 West Lake Avenue
Glenview, IL 60025
(847) 375-4733
(CNRN)

American Board of Perianesthesia Nursing Certification
475 Riverside Drive, 7th Floor
New York, NY 10115-0089
(800) 6AB-PANC (622-7262)
www.cpancapa.org
(CPAN, CAPA)

American Holistic Nurses' Certification Corporation
P.O. Box 845
Clarkdale, AZ 86324
(877) 284-0998
www.ahna.org
(HNC)

American Legal Nurse Consultant Certification Board
4700 West Lake Avenue
Glenview, IL 60025
(877) 402-2562
www.aalnc.org
(LNCC)

American Nurse-Midwifery Certification Council
8401 Corporate Drive, Suite 630
Landover, MD 20785
(301) 459-1321
www.accmidwife.org
(CNM)

American Nurses Credentialing Center
600 Maryland Avenue, SW, Suite 100 West
Washington, DC 20024-2571

(800) 284-2378
www.nursingworld.org/ancc
(C, CS, CAN, CNAA)

Board of Certification for Emergency Nursing
915 Lee Street
Des Plaines, IL 60016
(800) 243-8362
www.ena.org
(CEN, CFRN)

Board of Nephrology Examiners
P.O. Box 15945-282
Lanexa, KS 66285
(913) 541-9077 ext. 476
(CHN, CPDN)

Case Management Society of America
8201 Cantrell, Suite 230
Little Rock, AR 72227
(501) 225-2229
www.cmsa.org

Certification Board for Urologic Nurses and Associates
East Holly Avenue, Box 56
Pitman, NJ 08071-0056
(856) 256-2351
(CURN)

Certifying Board of Gastroenterology Nurses and Associates
3525 Ellicott Mills Drive, Suite N
Ellicott City, MD 21043-4547
(410) 418-4808
www.cbgna.org
(CGRN)

Childbirth Educators
2025 M Street, NW, Suite 800
Washington, DC 20036
(800) 368-4404
www.lamaze-childbirth.com
(ACCE, ICCE, CCE, ASPO/Lamaze)

Childbirth Education Preparation (CEP)
219 Central Avenue
Hatboro, PA 19040
(888) 344-9972
www.childbirtheducation.org

HIV/AIDS Nursing Certification Board (HANCB)
11250 Roger Bacon Drive, Suite B
Reston, VA 20190-5202
(703) 437-4377/ Fax: 435-4390
hancbl@aol.com
(ACRN)

Infusion Nurses Society
220 Norwood Park South
Norwood, MA 02062
(781) 440-9408
www.ins1.org
(CRNI)

International Nurses Society on Addictions (IntNSA)
1500 Sunday Drive, Suite 102
Raleigh, NC 27607
(919) 783-5871/ Fax: (919) 787-4916
www.intnsa.org
(CARN, CARN-AP)

NADONA/LTC Certification Registrar
10999 Reed Hartman Highway, Suite 233
Cincinnati, OH 45242-8301
(800) 222-0539
www.nadona.org
(Nurse Admin/Long-term Care- CDONA/LTC)

National Board of Certification of School Nurses
P.O. Box 1300
Scarborough, ME 04070-1300
(207) 883-2117
www.nasn.org
(CSN)

National Certification Board for Diabetes Educators
330 East Algonquin Road, Suite 4
Arlington Heights, IL 60605
(847) 228-9795
www.ncbde.org
(CDE)

**National Certifying Board for Ophthalmic
Registered Nurses** (CRNO)
1350 Broadway, 17th floor
New York, NY 10018
(212) 356-0660
www.ptcny.com

**National Certification Board of Pediatric Nurse
Practitioners and Nurses**
800 South Frederick Avenue, Suite 104
Gaithersburg, MD 20877-1450
www.pnpcert.org
(CPN, CPNP)

**National Certification Corporation for the Obstetric, Gynecologic
and Neonatal Nursing Specialties**
P.O. Box 11082
Chicago, IL 60611
(312) 951-0207
www.nccnet.org

**National Certification for the Obstetric, Gynecologic, and
Neonatal Nursing Specialties**
645 North Michigan Avenue, Suite 1058
Chicago, IL 60611
(800) 367-5613
(RNC)

National Commission on Correctional Health Care
1300 West Belmont Avenue
Chicago, IL 60657
(773) 880-1460
http://corrections.com/ncchc
(CCHP)

National League for Nursing (NLN)
61 Broadway
New York, NY 10006
(800) 669-1656
www.nln.org
Standardized Testing

Nephrology Nursing Certification Board
East Holly Avenue, Box 56
Pitman, NJ 08071-0056
(856) 256-2321
http://asprsn.inurse.com
(CNN)

New Concepts in Childbirth
698 Blue Ridge Drive
Medford, NY 11763

Oncology Nursing Certification Corp.
501 Holiday Drive
Pittsburgh, PA 15220-2759
(412) 921-7373
www.ons.org
(AOCN, OCN, CPON)

Orthopedic Nurses Certification Board (ONC)
East Holly Avenue, Box 56
Pitman, NJ 08071
(856) 256-2311
http://naon.inurse.com

Plastic Surgical Nursing Certification Board
East Holly Avenue, Box 56
Pitman, NJ 08071
(856) 256-2341
http://asprsn.inurse.com
(CPSN)

Rehabilitation Nursing Certification Board
4700 West Lake Avenue
Glenview, IL 60025
(800) 229-7530

www.rehabnurse.org
(CRRN-A)

Wound, Ostomy, and Continence Nursing Certification Board
1550 South Coast Highway, Suite 201
Laguna Beach, CA 92651
(913) 541-0400
www.wocncb.org
(CWOCN)

Appendix 3
Allied Health and Nursing Associations

Academy of Medical Surgical Nurses (AMSN)
East Holly Avenue, Box 56
Pitman, NJ 08071
(856) 256-2323/ Fax: (856) 589-7463
http://www.medsurgnurse.org

Aerospace Nursing Association
North Carolina Central University
Department of Nursing
P.O. Box 3369
Chapel Hill, NC 27514
(919) 560-6431/ Fax: (919) 560-5343
www.nursingcenter.com

Alliance for Psychosocial Nursing (APN)
6900 Grove Road
Thorofare, NJ 08086-9447
(856) 848-1000
http://www.psychnurse.org/

American Academy of Ambulatory Care Nursing (AACN)
East Holly Avenue, Box 56
Pitman, NJ 08071
(856) 256-08071/ Fax: (856) 589-7463
http://aaacn.inurse.com

American Academy of Nurse Practitioners (AANP)
P.O. Box 12846
Austin, TX 78711

(512) 442-4262/ Fax: (512) 442-6469
www.aanp.org

American Assembly for Men in Nursing (AAMN)
c/o NYSNA
11 Cornell Road
Latham, NY 12110
(346) 782-9400/ Fax: (346) 782-9530
www.ajn.org/ajnnet/nrsorgs/AAMN

American Association of Critical Care Nurses (AACN)
101 Columbia
Aliso Viejo, CA 92656
(949) 362-2000/ Fax: (949) 362-2020
www.aacn.org

American Association of Diabetes Educators (AADE)
444 North Michigan Avenue, Suite 1240
Chicago, IL 60611
(800) 338-3633
www.aadenet.org

American Association of Legal Nurse Consultants (AALNC)
4700 West Lake Avenue
Glenview, IL 0025
(877) 402-2562/ Fax: (847) 375-6313
www.aalnc.org

American Association of Managed Care Nurses, Inc. (AAMCN)
P.O. Box 4975
Glen Allen, VA 23058-4975
(804) 747-9698/ Fax (804) 747-5316
http://www.aamcn.org/

American Association of Neuroscience Nurses (AANN)
4700 West Lake Avenue
Glenview, IL 60025
(847) 375-4733/ Fax: (847) 375-4733
www.aann.org

American Association of Nurse Anesthetists (AANA)
222 South Prospect

Park Ridge, IL 60068
(847) 692-6968
www.aana.org

American Association of Nurse Attorneys
3525 Ellicott Drive, Suite N
Ellicott City, MD 21043-4547
(410) 418-4800/ Fax: (410) 418-4805
www.taana.org

American Association of Occupational Health Nurses (AAOH)
2920 Brandywine Road, Suite 100
Atlanta, GA 30341-4146
(770) 455-7757/ Fax: (770) 455-7271
www.aaohn.org

American Association of Perioperative Registered Nurses (AORN)
2170 South Parker Road, Suite 3000
Denver, CO 80231-5711
(800) 755-2676 or (303) 755-6300
www.aorn.org

American Association of Spinal Cord Injury Nurses (AASCIN)
75-20 Astoria Boulevard
Jackson Heights, NY 11370
(718) 803-3782 ext. 324/ Fax: (718) 803-0414
www.aascin.org

American Board for Occupational Health Nurses
201 East Ogden Road, Suite 114
Hinsdale, IL 60521-3652
(630) 789-5799/ Fax: (630) 789-8901
http://www.abohn.org/

American College of Nurse-Midwives
818 Connecticut Avenue, NW, Suite 900
Washington, DC 20006
(202) 728-9860/ Fax: (202) 728-9897
www.acnm.org

American College of Nurse Practitioners (ACNP)
503 Capitol Court, NE, Suite 300

Washington, DC 20002
(202) 659-2191/ Fax: (202) 659-2191
www.nurse.org/acnp

American Forensic Nurses
255 North El Cielo, Suite #195
Palm Springs, CA 92262
(760) 322-9925/ Fax: (760) 322-9914
www.amrn.com

American Holistic Health Association
P.O. Box 17400
Anaheim, CA 92817-7400
(714) 779-6152
www.healthworld.com/index2.htm

American Holistic Nurses Association
P.O. Box 2130
Flagstaff, AZ 86003-2130
(800) 278-2462/ Fax: (520) 526-2752
www.ahna.org

American Nephrology Nurses Association
East Holly Avenue, Box 56
Pitman, NJ 08071
(856) 256-2320/ Fax: (856) 589-7463
www.annanurse.org

American Nursing Informatics Association (ANIA)
10808 Foothill Boulevard, Suite 160
Rancho Cucamonga, CA 91730
www.ania.org

American Psychiatric Nurses Association
Colonial Place Three
2107 Wilson Boulevard, Suite 300-A
Arlington, VA 22201
(703) 243-2443/ Fax: (703) 243-3390
www.apna.org

American Public Health Association (APHA)
800 I Street, NW

Washington, DC 20001
(202) 777-2742/TTY: (202) 777-2500/ Fax: (202) 777-2534
www.apha.org

American Radiological Nurses Association (ARNA)
820 Jorie Boulevard
Oak Brook, IL 60523-2251
(630) 571-2670/ Fax: (630) 571-7837
http://www.rsna.org

American Society of Ophthalmic Registered Nurses (ASORN)
P.O. Box 193030
San Francisco, CA 94119
(415) 561-8513/ Fax: (415) 561-8531
http://webeye.ophth.uiowa.edu/asorn

American Society of Pain Management Nurses (ASPMN)
7794 Grow Drive
Pensacola, FL 32514
(850) 473-0233/ Fax: (850) 484-8762
www.aspmn.org

American Society of Perianesthesia Nurses (ASPAN)
10 Melrose Avenue, Suite 110
Cherry Hill, NJ 08003-3696
(856) 616-9600/ Fax: (856) 616-9600
Toll Free (877) 737-9696
www.aspan.org

American Society of Plastic and Reconstructive Surgical Nurses
(ASPRSN)
East Holly Avenue, Box 56
Pitman, NJ 08071
(856) 256-2340/ Fax: (856) 589-7463
http://asprsn.inurse.com

Association for Professionals in Infection Control and Epidemiology
(APIC)
1275 K Street, NW, Suite 1000
Washington, DC 20036
(202) 789-1890/ Fax: (202) 789-1899
www.apic.org

Association of Camp Nurses
8504 Thorsonveien NE
Bemidji, MN 56601
(218) 586-2633
http://www.campnurse.org/contact.html
(CAN)

Association of Medical Professionals with Hearing Losses (AMPHL)
1216 Timber Hawk Trail
Dayton, OH 45458
www.AMPHL.org

Association of Nurses in AIDS Care
80 South Summit Street
500 Courtyard Square
Akron, OH 44308
(800) 260-6780/ Fax: (330) 762-5813
www.anacnet.org

Association of Occupational Health Professionals (AOHP)
11250 Roger Bacon Drive, Suite 8
Reston, VA 20190-5202
(800) 362-4347/ Fax: (703) 435-4390
www.aohp.org/aohp

Association of Operating Room Nurses
2170 South Parker Road, Suite 300
Denver, CO 80231-5711
(303) 755-6300
http://jeffline.tju.edu/hcg/hcg-financial/8a-financialp91.htm

Association of Preoperative Nurses (AORN)
2170 South Parker Road, Suite 300
Denver, CO 80231
(800) 755-2676/ Fax: (303) 750-2927
www.aorn.org

Association of Pediatric Oncology Nurses (APON)
4700 West Lake Avenue
Glenview, IL 60025
(847) 375-4724/ Fax: (877) 734-8755
www.apon.org

Association of Rehabilitation Nurses (ARN)
4700 West Lake Avenue
Glenview, IL 60025
(800) 229-7530 or (847) 375-4710/ Fax: (877) 734-9384
www.rehabnurse.org

Association of Women's Health, Obstetric, and Neonatal Nurses
(AWHONN)
2000 L Street, NW, Suite 740
Washington, DC 20036
(800) 673-8499/ Fax: (202) 728-0575
www.awhonn.org

Dermatology Nurses Association (DNA)
East Holly Avenue, Box 56
Pitman, NJ 08071
(856) 256-2330/ Fax: (856) 589-7463
http://dna.insurse.com

Developmental Disabilities Nurses Association (DDNA)
228 Grimes Street, Suite 246
Eugene, OR 97402
(800) 888-6733/ Fax: (360) 332-2280
www.ddna.org

Emergency Nurses Association (ENA)
915 Lee Street
Des Plaines, IL 60016-6569
(800) 900-9659/ Fax: (847) 460-4001
http://www.ena.org/

Home Healthcare Nurses Association
228 7th Street, SE
Washington, DC 20333
(800) 558-4462/ Fax: (202) 547-3540
www.hhna.org

Hospice and Palliative Nurses Association (HPNA)
Medical Center East
211 North Whitfield Street, Suite 375
Pittsburgh, PA 15206-3031
(412) 787-9301/ Fax: (412) 787-9305
www.hpna.org

International Parish Nurse Resource Center
205 North Touhy, Suite 124
Park Ridge, IL 60068
(800) 556-5368/ Fax: (847) 692-5109
http://www.advocatehealth.com/about/faith/parishn/index2.html

International Society of Nurses in Genetics
7 Haskins Road
Hanover, NH 03755
(603) 643-5706
http://nursing.creighton.edu/isong/

International Transplant Nurses Society
1739 East Carson Street, Box 351
Pittsburgh, PA 15203-1900
(412) 488-0240/ Fax: (412) 431-5911
www.itns.org

Infusion Nurses Society (INS)
220 Norwood Park South
Norwood, MA 02062
(781) 440-9408/ Fax: (781) 440-9409
www.ins1.org

Medical-Legal Consulting Institute
2476 Bolsover Street
Houston, TX 77005
(800) 880-0944
www.legalnurse.com

National Association for Health Care Recruitment (NAHCR)
P.O. Box 531107
Orlando, FL 32853-1107
(407) 843-6981/ Fax: (407) 423-4648
www.nahcr.com

National Association of Directors of Nursing Administration in Long Term Care
10101 Alliance Road, Suite 140
Cincinnati, OH 45242
(800) 222-0539/ Fax: (513) 791-3699
www.nadona.org

National Association of Hispanic Nurses
1501 16th Street, NW
Washington, DC 20036
(202) 387-2477/ Fax: (202) 483-7183
http://www.thehispanicnurses.org/

National Association of Neonatal Nurses
701 Lee Street, Suite 450
Des Plaines, IL 60016
(847) 375-3660 or (800) 451-3795/ Fax: (888) 477-6266
www.nann.org

National Association of Orthopedic Nurses (NAON)
East Holly Avenue, Box 56
Pitman, NJ 08071-0056
(856) 256-2310/ Fax: (856) 589-7463
http://naon.inurse.com

National Association of Pediatric Nurse Associates and Practitioners
(NAP-NAP)
20 Brace Road, Suite 200
Cherry Hill, NJ 08034-2633
(877) 662-7627 or (856) 857-9700/ Fax: (856) 857-1600
www.napnap.org

National Association of School Nurses
P.O. Box 1300
Scarborough, ME 04070
(207) 883-2117/ Fax: (207) 883-2683
www.nasn.org

National Black Nurses Association
8630 Fenton Street, Suite 330
Silver Spring, MD 20910-3803
(301) 589-3200/ Fax: (301) 589-3223
http://www.nbna.org/

National Nurses Society on Addictions (NNSA)
1500 Sunday Drive, Suite 102
Raleigh, NC 27607
(919) 783-5871/ Fax: (919) 787-4916
www.intnsa.org

National Organization for Associate Degree Nursing
11250 Roger Bacon Drive, Suite 8
Reston, VA 20190-5202
(703) 437-4377
http://www.noadn.org/

National Student Nurses Association (NSNA)
555 West 57th Street, Suite 1327
New York, NY 10019
(212) 581-2211/ Fax: (212) 581-2368
www.nsna.org

North American Nursing Diagnosis Association (NANDA)
1211 Locust Street
Philadelphia, PA 19107
(800) 647-9002/ Fax: (215) 545-8107
www.nanda.org

Nurses Organization of Veterans Affairs
1726 M Street, NW, Suite 1101
Washington, DC 20036
(202) 296-0888/ Fax: (202) 833-1577
www.vanurse.org/cgi-bin/vpecgi.exe/VA-Nurse.AEF58274B7CA890
D4E0C349E/auto_start.html

Oncology Nursing Society (ONS)
501 Holiday Drive
Pittsburgh, PA 15220-2749
(412) 921-7373/ Fax: (412) 921-6565
www.ons.org

Society of Gastroenterology Nurses and Associates (SGNA)
401 North Michigan Avenue
Chicago, IL 60611
(800) 245-7462 or, in IL (312) 321-5165/ Fax: (312) 527-6658
www.sgna.org

Society of Otorhinolary and Head-Neck Nurses (SOHN)
116 Canal Street, Suite A
New Smyrna Beach, FL 32168
(386) 428-1695/ Fax: (386) 423-7566
www.sohnnurse.com

Society of Pediatric Nurses
7794 Grow Drive
Pensacola, FL 32514
(800) 723-2902/ Fax: (850) 484-8762
www.pedsnurses.org

Society of Urologic Nurses and Associates (SUNA)
East Holly Avenue, Box 56
Pitman, NJ 08071-0056
(856) 256-2335/ Fax: (856) 589-7463
http://suna.inurse.com

Transcultural Nursing Society
36600 Schoolcraft Road
Livonia, MI 48150-1173
(888) 432-5470 (toll free), or
(734) 432-5470/ Fax: (734) 432-5463
http://www.tcns.org/

Wound, Ostomy, and Continence Nurses Society (WOCN)
4700 West Lake Avenue
Glenview, IL 60025
(888) 224-9626/ Fax: (866) 615-8560
www.wocn.org

NursingCenter.com
www.nursingcenter.com/resources/organization_list.cfm?purview_
id=3

Index

Acknowledgments

For many years, career counselors at the University of Pennsylvania have been compiling resources for nursing students and alumni. I am fortunate that, during my tenure at Penn, the University of Pennsylvania Press (specifically Patricia Smith, the former social science editor) suggested that a nursing job search handbook might be useful. I am in the pleasant position of building on the work and resources accumulated by my predecessors Rachel Brown, Ann Glusker, Donna Kahn Patkin, Deborah Gould, and Peggy Curchack. After I developed a plan for the book's content and completed a first draft, Dr. Neville Strumpf, Edith Clemmer Steinbright Professor of Gerontology, and Dr. Kathleen McCauley, Associate Professor of Cardiovascular Nursing, generously gave of their time to read and comment on it; in so doing they encouraged me to continue with the project.

Current staff members in the University of Pennsylvania Career Services Office lent their support and help. I especially appreciate the recent contributions of my colleagues Leslie Trimble and Donna Kahn Patkin, who prepared, read, and evaluated sample materials. Thanks, too, for Cristen Gilbert's work to incorporate formatting and materials changes. My teammates Mary Heiberger and Julia Vick read the final draft of the manuscript and offered helpful suggestions. My thanks to all.

Two other groups have been essential to the effort. The book's written materials are based on the language and disciplines of the nurses with whom I have worked at Penn. I learned a great deal from them. Their resumes inspired the book's models and their dilemmas generated questions that I attempted to answer through text, resources, or sample written materials. My accumulated knowledge in career services and specific work with nurses at the University of Pennsylvania are the experiences on which my recommendations are based. This book was born and designed to address the needs of nursing students and practitioners within and outside academic communities.

Thanks to the professionals at the University of Pennsylvania Press, Jo Joslyn, acquisitions editor, who shepherded the project along and who guided me kindly through the publishing process, and Noreen O'Connor, who carefully edited the final version.

Special thanks to my husband, Christopher, who is my mainstay.